The Touring Musician's Survival Guide

ROSS CRAIB

Copyright © 2019 by Ross Craib Music
www.rosscraibdrums.com

All rights reserved. This eBook is protected by international copyright law. You may only use it if you have bought a licensed version from www.rosscraibdrums.com or an authorised reseller. No part of this publication may be reproduced, distributed, or transmitted in any form or by any means, including photocopying, recording, or other electronic or mechanical methods, without the prior written permission of the publisher, except in the case of brief quotations embodied in critical reviews and certain other non commercial uses permitted by copyright law. For permission requests, write to the publisher, addressed "Attention: Permissions" at the address below.

This eBook is Published by Ross Craib Music
Ross Craib Music, 5 Fairlawn Avenue, London W4 5EF

Although the author and publisher have made every effort to ensure that the information in this book was correct at press time, the author and publisher do not assume and hereby disclaim any liability to any party for any loss, damage, or disruption caused by errors or omissions, whether such errors or omissions result from negligence, accident, or any other cause.

ISBN: 978-1-5272-5595-1

Table of Contents:

ABOUT THE AUTHOR 1

Introduction 3

First Things First 5

Preparation 9
    Tour Management 9
    Gear 12
    Rehearsal 15
    Packing for Tour 18

Lifestyle 21
    Transport 22
    Sleeper Buses 23
    International Tours 28
    Be Productive 31
    Timings 32

Attitude 35
    Money 36
    Remember why you are there. 38
    Remember why you started playing music in the first place 40
    Know your chain of command 44

Health 49
    Diet 49

    Food 51

    Alcohol 54

    Sleep 57

    Fitness 58

    Mental Health 60

    Burnout 70

Getting the gig & Networking 77

    What is networking? 77

    The road to the biggest gig of my career: 80

    Networking On Tour 83

    Musical Directors 84

    Money and Rates 91

Money Management 97

    What does 'claiming' mean? 98

    What is claimable? 99

    Invoicing 101

    Business you and Personal you 102

Support Slots 105

Quick-fire Questions 109

Advice from the Pro's 127

Post Tour 145

Conclusion 149

Thank You 150

References 151

The Touring Musician's Survival Guide

ABOUT THE AUTHOR

Ross Craib

Arriving in London to study music in 2010, professional musician Ross Craib immersed himself in the London music scene. He has since climbed the ranks and 9 years on, boasts an impressive CV having performed on a Top 5 Official UK Album, 4 BBC Radio 1 singles, The Graham Norton Show, Main Stages at some of the worlds biggest festivals and opening the Olympics Ceremony in London 2012.

It has not been an easy road by any stretch of the imagination, however as most musicians will tell you – overcoming the struggles make the successes even sweeter.

Having embarked on 10+ International tours across more than 20 countries, Ross felt it was time to share some of his experiences and stories from the road that could benefit other musicians about to take the leap into professional music with aspirations of touring.

Currently on tour with singer-songwriter dodie, Ross has a busy touring schedule and is set to head out on tour number 8 with her throughout 2020/21.

Introduction

After answering similar repeated questions from friends, family and colleagues about what it's like to go on tour, I decided to sit down and try to explain in the simplest terms what can be expected for the modern day musician in 2019.

Welcome to a very honest publication about the challenges and expectations of a modern day musician on tour and some of the complex relationships and situations you may come across during your time on the road.

Covering everything from preparation and attitude to lifestyle and networking, the concept behind The Touring Musician's Survival Guide is to educate younger, aspiring or existing musicians about the realities of a life on tour; What to expect, to watch out for, to maintain, to do, to learn...all with the aims of making you a more well rounded, equipped and employable musician in today's industry.

Written by musicians for musicians from first hand experience, consider me your checklist, your first aid kit, your careers advisor and your life coach all rolled into one step-by-step musical manual.

Welcome to the Touring Musician's Survival Guide!

First Things First

Before we delve into the how to survive a life on tour, it is important to acknowledge why we do it in the first place.

Touring is big business!

Artists go on tour for a multitude of reasons, but the main overarching factor is the fan base! Music is International; fans stream and buy music from every corner of the globe, so it would be foolish not to visit these target markets with the aims of capitalising on the other viable income streams aside from record sales; These include ticket sales, booking fees, merchandise, signings and appearances.

It gives the fans the chance to see their favourite artists live and it is important to give back to them; These are the people that will keep careers afloat, so it is important to cherish every single person who supports your craft.

In a nutshell, touring is about making money and maintaining an audience with the aims of building a sustainable and long lasting career.

When an artist tours, they will need a band, a crew and a team. If done correctly it can become the biggest source of revenue for all involved. Touring in itself is a big business and for some people, their only business - in a successful economy, live music serves not only the fans, the artists and the musicians, but it can also generate many other jobs, allowing our ever changing music scene to thrive;

> *In 2016, UK Music released an online document showing live music in the UK alone generated £4 Billion in music tourism revenue creating close to 50,000 full time music jobs and these figures have been on the rise ever since!*

As long as there is demand, musicians will *and should* always tour to ensure they enjoy a slice of this increasing and very much thriving musical 'pie'!

...So, now that we've gotten the generic reasons and business foundations as to why musicians tour out of the way, it's time to get stuck in to the real life elements surrounding a tour and focus on you!

The further we delve into this book, the more you will evaluate your own reasons for performing and touring and how *you* would like to succeed at it!

My aim is to give you the insider knowledge needed to tailor your own happiness around this industry's chaotic lifestyle, by arming you with the most important information I've learnt along the way.

The Touring Musician's Survival Guide is here to serve you – take from it what you wish and survive in this game the best way you can!

Without further ado...Chapter 1!

Preparation

"By failing to prepare, you are preparing to fail."

Benjamin Franklin

It's confirmed...you've got the gig and you're all booked up to go on tour! But, where do you start? Preparation in this game is key! It'll bode for a much nicer time away and hopefully remove a lot of the stresses before you even set foot on that bus.

Tour Management

For those on bigger tours – it's likely you will have a designated Tour Manager (TM) who will take care of all things business on the road; Their job is essentially to ensure the smooth running of a tour from start to finish – This can be achieved by ensuring all of the 'advance' work is completed to a high standard before setting off.

It is important to note, the TM will likely be acting as tour accountant and responsible for all money coming in and going out, therefore, before a Tour can even commence, there will need to be a budget put in place; This is also the role of the TM to present to the artist or band's management before any contracts are signed. If the costs are too high, the TM will search to offer more viable solutions.

Once the budget is set, the advance work will commence; This will include things like sending tech specs to venues, booking travel arrangements & accommodation, organising rehearsals and schedules, dealing with tour vendors (lights, audio, backline & transport), securing tour documents (VISA's, laminates & security passes) and learning venue information, including timings (noise curfews, bus parking, arrival / load in etc.).

To ensure smooth operations they will be liaising with everyone from venue managers, promoters and travel agents to accountants, management, label, crew and band.

Once on tour, the TM will oversee travel arrangements, ensure the safety of band and artist, organise Per Diem's*, food buyouts and catering, settle performance fees, oversee any promotional activities, prepare day sheets with all timings etc.

Per Diems (PD's) are a daily amount of money paid to the touring party to cover all living expenses.

The list is endless and all of these seemingly simple tasks can add up - A good tour manager will be your best friend and saviour on a long run! They will be your point of call for all things non-musical – if you have any queries or stresses along the way, you can and should be able to trust your TM with sensitive subjects.

It is possible your TM may also have another technical job on the tour, such as front of house engineer or driver, however this varies from tour to tour.

If you are on a smaller tour, it would still be advisable to get someone to TM, even if a member of the band or engineer. There's a saying - *"The more you sweat in peace, the less you'll bleed in war"* - the tour will be a hell of a lot smoother with all these details in place and ensure there are no curve balls upon arrival...and trust me, even with the best tour manager in the game...there will ALWAYS be curve balls.

dodie band & TM, Elliot Taylor in black, Pre Stage @ The Roundhouse 2019

Photo by Parri Thomas

Gear

Once all the details are set, the next thing on the agenda should be your gear; It will be your musical voice on the road and it needs to be robust, sound great and prepared for any eventuality.

Make sure you've invested in protective casing – soft bags are great for local gigs, but a good heavy duty flight case can save you a ton of money in the long run; I stupidly toured a mixer in a soft case one time...needless to say it didn't last long. When you're buying an expensive item, you should always factor in the protection it needs to ensure longevity. You wouldn't buy a house without insurance – the same should be said for the tools of your trade. Speaking of which – get some musical instrument insurance too! If you join the Musician's Union, you automatically receive £2,000 worth of instrument insurance, along with public liability and all of their other perks. There are of course alternatives, but this is a good place to start.

(Remember to number and label everything!)

Before you set off be sure to freshen up your gear; new strings, skins, sticks, cables etc...Any older or temperamental accessories, squeaky pedals or things that rattle or buzz...anything that niggles you, basically – renew it! There's nothing worse than a breakage or repeated irritation mid-set to ruin the flow or enjoyment of your show...or worse, ruin it for the audience.

Don't just assume everything will be fine with these items – You want to ensure *you* are the best possible choice for an artist – both in ability and economy! If something goes wrong during rehearsals or shows that is preventable, the people in charge will just see you causing problems, which in turn takes up more time, looks unprofessional and costs more money!

Smaller items can get lost or damaged on tours...with multiple bands and hundreds of cases kicking about, it's only a matter of time before something goes awry, so try to have spares for the majority of smaller or essential items, where possible! *(from a drummer's perspective: skins, Moon gel, felts, clutches, sticks, leads for electronics etc. Guitarists: picks, leads, strings... etc.)*

If you are working with backing tracks, make sure you have a show backup - This could be a laptop or playback unit. If you are running click and monitors through in-ears, make sure they are up for the job and you have a reserve pair or cable in case of breakage.

If you are in need of some new gear, reach out to the companies you enjoy playing – they may be able to help you with recommendations and may even offer some form of artist discounts; This won't always happen, but if you don't ask, you won't get. It also allows you to strike up a connection and start a relationship from the outset with great brands. I've been fortunate enough to work with some of my favourite companies over the years, but most of these relationships had to be cultivated over many years with emails back and fourth simply keeping people up to date on what I was up to!

It can seem costly up front, but it is your voice on stage and you want it to shine. If you look after your gear, it'll look after you! Protect yourself by being prepared.

Idea: Make a Gear checklist – with all the chaos that's going on in the venues, it'll make things a lot smoother and you'll be able to see immediately if something is missing.

Rehearsal

Practice makes perfect

There's no two ways about it...Your dream gig isn't just going to happen overnight! It takes time, effort and hard work to hone your skills to a level that will warrant successful touring and great performances. This is true at any level of music, whether competing in a local battle of the bands, sitting a graded exam or auditioning for the latest chart topping artist. If you put the effort in, you will reap the rewards!

Rehearsal Rule No.1

Be on time and always come as prepared as possible to day 1 of band rehearsals; This is not the time to learn and any blaggers will stand out like a sore thumb in a professional environment.

There is a difference between practice and rehearsal! Practice is running through the songs learning them step by step...Rehearsal is preparing for the live show – everything from choreographed movements and visuals right through to the script. Of course the scope for spontaneity will exist, but this only comes with the comfort of having a fully rehearsed and well oiled show!

Personally, I like to practice alone the weeks leading up to rehearsals and where possible, meet the Musical Director (MD) to discuss musical options and any technical information.

For example: Are we using samples or acoustics in this section? What kind of instrumentation do you want on this track? Are there any interesting arrangements that are going to be tried out? What is the provisional set list order? Etc.

(Note: In many cases the MD will also be the guy who gave you the gig by putting the band together for the artist. See Chapter 5.)

If you want to maintain a good reputation, go above and beyond where possible – make your parts interesting and musical and suggest different options to the MD or artist if you think they benefit the live arrangement of the song.

Arrangements are always subject to change and new ideas will be introduced, so try not to overcomplicate your parts or overplay – remember your job as a musician is to support the music and the song as a whole! You also want the tour to be enjoyable, not stressful; There will be a lot of information to take on board and the last thing you want to worry about is the thing that comes easy to you. Overplaying is also detrimental to the song and just bad practice all round.

Most importantly, be flexible with a 'can-do' attitude; This is no place to be stubborn or precious, especially if you are being paid as a session musician.

Be patient; Rehearsals can take time. There may be changes to be made to the programming if you are running backing tracks or if using wireless in-ear monitoring, there may be frequency interference issues. With lots of moving parts and with most artists using newer technologies, problems will inevitably arise – rehearsal exists to iron out creases, so you have to learn to just chill, go with it and help where possible!

Be respectful to the other musicians; Don't noodle on the guitar when somebody is talking or play a drum solo when the guitarist is running some chords. Try to avoid distractions and always be 'in the room'. Unless you are using your phone for charts or to record the rehearsal, put it away.

Guitarists, learn the drum grooves...Drummers, learn the chords. Everyone, learn the lyrics – these are tools that will help you and ensure you are fully prepared. If you've rehearsed enough, it will allow you to enjoy the show along with the audience and the other band members.

If there is anything you are uncomfortable with, speak up! It's better to run and re-run the parts in a safe environment before you head out on tour. The other musicians will understand – they want this show to be as good as it can too and they will respect your eagerness to get it right. The same goes for the other members – support them if they need help.

The first show will come round at a million miles an hour and as soon as you step out on that stage, the show ain't stopping for no-one except the artist.

Photo credit: Samuel Morris
Dodie rehearsal 2019

Packing for Tour

This will vary depending on what kind of tour you are on and what kind of routines you have, but one constant remains the same; you will be living out of a suitcase for a definite amount of time, so be prepared for speed & efficiency.

I like to have 2 bags on tour; One which is small enough to carry around with essentials like in-ears, laptop, chargers, a daily change of clothes etc. The other a large enough suitcase to hold clean clothes for at least 2 weeks.

On a longer run there will come a time where you'll have to do laundry – some venues will have facilities, or you will have to source a laundromat.

Everyone on a tour has their different routines and packing rituals, so until you embark on your first run and make some mistakes, it's hard to be fully prepared in advance. Some of the best hacks I've found are the small things:

- *Bring 2 phone chargers – one for your bunk on the bus, one for daily use. Label EVERYTHING – think how many iphone cables will be on a tour bus!*

- *Always have a laundry bag or clothes divider so you know what is clean / dirty.*

- *Tour bus temperatures can vary dramatically so always have a selection of comfy layered clothes for travelling.*

- *Bring ear plugs or noise cancelling headphones.*

- *For splitter tours, bring a pillow!*

- *Toiletries for most eventualities (inc. medications & vitamins)*

- *Multivitamins to prevent illness are a must*

- *PASSPORT (Just thought I'd remind you)*

- *A prepaid debit card, such as Monzo or Revolut – these can be topped up on your phone and offer better rates on currency than your everyday bank*

etc....

Lifestyle

"If you organize your life around your passion, you can turn your passion into your story and then turn your story into something bigger - something that matters."

Blake Mycoskie

Music is one of those beautiful phenomenons that brings people from all cultures, nationalities and backgrounds together. It allows us as musicians to cross borders and travel to far off places to share our message and talents with others. It is a way of life and if successful, a great way to live that life.

From the outside looking in, all of this might seem wonderfully glamorous and *rock 'n roll*, but be aware this life isn't for everyone! Don't get me wrong, I love it, but you have to be prepared for some sacrifice along the way.

Succeeding in music requires dedication and focus to set your sights on the bigger picture; It requires a lot of hard work, time, energy and (often) money to get to where you wish to be! Late nights and long hours, practicing, travelling, gigging, studying, watching, stressing, questioning...Then again, if you're reading this book, you probably already have a passion for music and have faced at least one of these hurdles in your tenure!

Transport

There are many ways to get around on tour, but the most common encounters will be with splitter van's or sleeper buses.

Say goodbye to your creature comforts.

You will be living in very close proximity with your colleagues for weeks on end; With space for up to 15 other people on a sleeper bus or sharing hotel rooms (*sometimes even beds*) on splitter tours, you have to be a people-person with an open mind!

With everyone's different routines and sleeping patterns, you need to have a chilled attitude. Understand when people need their space and try not to retaliate if someone gets a bit grumpy – everyone will have a day where their fuze is just a bit too short. Privacy is a rare thing on tour and sensitivity is much appreciated.

Sleeper Buses

Unwritten rule – if someone is in their bunk with their curtain closed – this is essentially a 'do not disturb' sign.

If you are tall like me (6'4) a tour bus will not be your friend; Get used to hitting your head on most things and - for the guys - peeing with your head against the wall for stability on a moving vehicle. Saying this – US tour buses tend to be single decker, meaning a bit more room for tall people! European buses, not so much.

It's probably good at this stage to note the toilet rule on a sleeper bus – No solids! Get used to having a routine of using the facilities in the venues before getting on the bus.* I've heard nightmare stories of the toilet blocking, overflowing and destroying everyone's suitcases after filtering into the bay of the bus...don't be that guy!
(Pre-stage nerves usually take care of this business)

The water on a bus is stored in a tank and you can only imagine the last time it was cleaned...Therefore, it is undrinkable and we use bottled water for everything!
e.g Brushing teeth, boiling kettle etc.

Go Green! On our last run we ordered all waters from the promoter to be from recyclable cans – not a single plastic bottle in sight for 6 weeks! You'd be amazed at how many plastic bottles a touring crew gets through in 6 weeks.

Bunk sizes may vary very slightly from top to bottom, so try and get on early on day one to pick one with enough leg and head room – this can seem a bit fickle, so be subtle about it. This will be your effective bedroom for the duration of the tour, so try to keep it tidy without too much clutter. If you are lucky enough to have a 'junk bunk'* on the bus, you can throw bags, shoes, coats etc. in there...on the flip side, to avoid cluttering the communal areas, you may have to sleep with them – So try to pack your overnight essentials wisely!

Picture: (Left) the inside of a bunk , (Right) the sleeping quarters on a sleeper bus with bunks either side, 3x3, (taken from personal archives.)

***A junk bunk is a spare bed on a tour bus that is not being used**

**Heads up - Make sure you sleep with your feet in the direction of travel...if the driver breaks too hard, it it will only be your feet thumping into the wall, and not your head.

***Sleep in the death bunks at your own discretion – top & front above the driver. Named this way because of danger from low bridges etc.

Tour buses are effectively 24hr hotels, with people sleeping at different times of day! Be respectful at all times, even in the middle of the afternoon. Tour bus drivers sleep on the bus in their own section when the bus is parked up - If you are awake, they are likely asleep! Don't go slamming doors, cranking the music or having a rowdy FIFA footie tournaments unless you want a tired bus driver who is responsible for your safety.

Common sense – If you are the last off the bus, make sure you close and lock the door behind you; You'd be surprised how many strangers try to pop their head inside a bus and with all the valuables on board, it would make a pretty successful hunting ground for thieves.

Regards bringing guests on the bus – this is usually a bit of a no-no, but if they do come on, make sure they stay in the lounge and don't venture into the sleeping quarters where valuables live and tired band or crew members may be chilling. Never transport guests from one city to another, unless otherwise agreed with the people in charge.

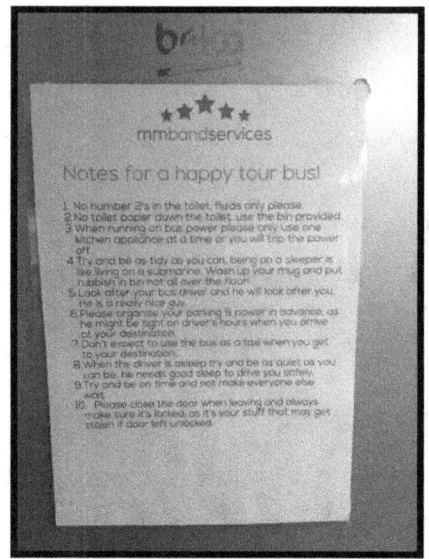 

*Left: The common Sleeper Bus rules
(Taken by Ross Craib on MM Band Services 2019 bus)*

Right: our 14 berth US tour bus sleeping quarters (2019)

Showering on a bus tour is a bit of a russian roulette; Even though many buses have a shower in them, you will rarely use them. Instead, you will be using venue facilities and you never know what you're going to get until you reach the green room. We've started ranking showers on a scale of 1-10 with inclusive factors such as temperature, water pressure and cleanliness. It can make a grim experience at least a little bit more amusing by laughing at just how bad it is with one another.

Some touring members will choose to source local gyms or swimming baths for showering if the facilities are not up to scratch.

On days off, you will likely have 'day rooms' in hotels to shower in, and if on a bigger budget tour – you may have hotel rooms a lot more often if staying overnight in a city.

Splitter touring will of course differ and you will be sleeping in hotel rooms every night, with nicer shower facilities; When there are perks to these luxuries, the downside is the following day of travel - Waking up early for bus call to sit in a van for X amount of hours can get exhausting and you may not feel as relaxed by the time you arrive at the venue for load in and soundcheck.

Splitter tour - Martin Luke Brown – 2015

Left to right: Chris Ketley, Ido Tavori, Charlie Fowler, Mikey Fowler, Martin Luke Brown and myself

There's not too much advice I can give on these tours...you will be sitting in a seat for every journey, so bring whatever you can to make this more comfortable. Eg. A Pillow, DVD's, books, lots of music & headphones.

The method of transport will be decided upon budget and the number of touring crew. People will generally prefer one or the other; Personally I like tour buses – it's nice to know you can walk out of one venue straight onto your *hotel* and wake up at the next.

International Tours

Finally, if you are touring internationally you will have to take flights and ferries at some point. As most of the population has flown before, I'll skip the obvious, but a few things to note:

VISA's or other work permits and documents – get them...and get them in advance! It is a terrible idea to travel or work without the correct paperwork, as along with jeopardising your travel plans and shows, you risk deportation with a lifetime ban on returning in certain countries. US VISA's are notoriously long-winded, so make sure to secure these as far in advance as possible leading up to a tour; We had to postpone a show a few years ago due to the length of time the process took, even after we had submitted all the paperwork and attended our interviews well in advance!

Be careful when booking travel insurance as a musician – music is deemed 'manual labour' and is therefore exempt from most standard insurance policies. Read the small print! Lots of policies also only cover up to 30 days out of the country and require you to begin and end your 'trip' in the UK; This would mean if you are touring for longer than 30 days, your insurance cover would become invalid. Opt instead to purchase a good music or entertainment insurance broker that offers year long cover with trips of up to 6 months out of the country; That means if your dream world tour gig comes in you should have nothing to worry about, except touching down in the UK once a year! These policies only cost between £100-200 and they cover instruments as well!

A good airport hack is to invest in membership or credit cards that offer 'lounge access'. There are a couple of different cards available, including Priority Pass and Dragon Pass, amongst others. These grant you access to the private lounges in most major airports around the world that provide free food and drinks, comfier, more relaxing surroundings and sometimes showers (great if you have a connection and need to freshen up or kill some time). These are only worth the investment if you fly regularly though, as they are a little expensive.

Buy some handheld scales to weigh your bag before getting to the airport! If you don't have these, try to arrive a little bit earlier to scope out an unattended check-in desk where you can weigh your bag beforehand – proceed with caution as it's frowned upon. Your allowance will usually be 23kg.

If your flight is cancelled, don't automatically accept a refunded ticket – this will essentially take the airline out of 'your pocket' and they will be done with you, leaving you on your own to book your travel once again. I did this recently and learnt the hard way! If you hold on to your ticket, however, and are still booked with the airline, they have a duty of care to look after you – e.g. offering accommodation, upgrades on the next flight they put you on, wait-listing you for the next available flight out or offering alternative routes.

In regards ferries - It is forbidden for anyone to stay in parked vehicles during sail for safety reasons, however that doesn't mean we haven't done it; In the past on early morning journeys after big nights out, we have opted to stay on the bus and see it through, however, after hearing about a lorry driver who did the same and was crushed to death in choppy seas in 2018, it's just not worth it.

If that doesn't put you off...for the claustrophobic members out there - just remember you are trapped in a bus with no lights, electricity, air conditioning or running water until the ferry docks and the driver comes back in anything up to 4 hours time.

Be Productive

You will have a lot of downtime on tour, so try to be efficient. It is very easy to be lazy, but try to set yourself tasks. If you have some invoicing to do, do it! If you fancy writing or finishing off a half written song, do it! Need to update your website...you get it! You are being paid by the artist for your time, but you are not needed 24/7, so make the most of this opportunity and try to capitalise.

If you have friends in cities you haven't seen in years, use this opportunity to meet them - This is one of the luxuries of being a touring musician.

If you've never been to a city before, wake up early to explore it; It's very easy to wake up late and spend an entire tour stuck inside the venue – don't look back on the tour thinking "I wish I'd seen that".

If there are other local musician's or artists you've been wishing to collaborate with, or you've become internet friends and bonded over a mutual interest, hit them up! It will be just as exciting for them as it is for you to bring something fresh to their area! This can also bring opportunity and meetings of chance that may spark further career prospects or great friendships!

If there are any musician's or teachers you look up to or you've really wanted to get advice from, get in touch and try to book a lesson or see if they're willing to let you buy them lunch so you can pick their brain about things.

You might have hobbies or interests such as sports, culture, history etc. Get out there and watch some ice hockey, basketball or baseball game...go to a museum, take some sightseeing tours! Personally, I like tattoo's, so when on tour I try to get small pieces from artists that I like and follow online. I would never have the chance otherwise simply due to distance, so I try to capitalise...plus it makes for a great story.

Don't be scared to try local cuisine's! You never know when you may come back to this country, so push the boat out and try new things! You might hate it...you might discover your new favourite dish!

Timings

With such tight schedules on a tour, it is good to be aware of the kind of 'calls' you are going to see on the day sheet. *(The day sheet is the daily schedule that will list all timings for band and crew and is usually prepared by the TM).*

Lobby Call – Only applicable if staying in hotels; The time all band and crew have to be ready to leave the hotel.
Load In / Load Out – This will also usually have all technical details for crew eg. Is it a flat push to stage or are there stairs to navigate, how many local crew will be there etc.

Band Call – This will be the time the band are expected to be ready for soundcheck.

Dinner – If catering is provided, this will often be at a set time. Usually after soundcheck.

Doors + support times

Stage Time

Curfew – all music must be stopped by this time.

Venue Cleared – the time all members have to exit the venue.

Bus Call – The time the bus will leave for the next destination.

Timings are all subject to change, however, it is highly advisable you never miss them unless you wish to annoy every other member waiting for you. If you foresee a problem for whatever reason, let the TM know immediately. The artist is really the only person who can delay bus call, but unforeseen circumstances can always happen.

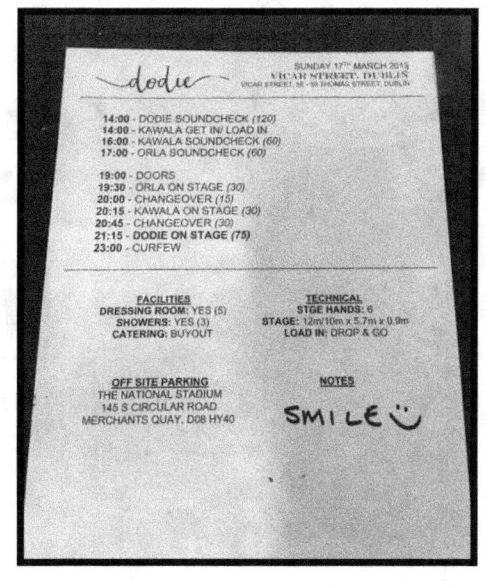

Example day sheet Taken from personal phone archives – dodie tour 2019

I've been guilty of missing an early bus call one time due to oversleeping – long story short, I got left behind and had to make my own way on my own dime from Sicily to London. In fairness the TM did everything he could to reach me, but for the sake of the rest of the touring party, they had to leave to catch their flight from the closest airport – 3 hours away! As ashamed of missing it as I am...it goes to prove just how strict certain calls can be, and I learnt my lesson the hard...and expensive way!

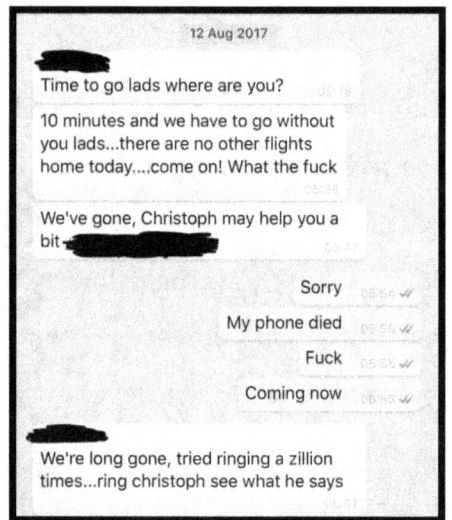

Learning my lesson the hard way

Taken from the archives of a tour group chat on Whatsapp - 2017

Attitude

*"It is your attitude, not your aptitude,
that determines your altitude"*

Zig Ziglar

The way you act on a tour is the single most important and employable attribute you possess. Closely followed by your musical abilities, of course. Out of a 24hr day you might spend a maximum of 4 hours on stage – the rest of the time you are just hanging out; Nobody wants to be surrounded by downbeat people, so ask yourself what kind of person you are and what you can bring to a team.

You don't have to be the joker...you could be the caring, sensitive one..or the efficient one who likes to organise fun activities. Whoever you are, just be yourself...but try to be the most positive version of that self. Try to make decisions which are going to benefit the whole team and not just yourself. Negativity spreads like wildfire and is the worst thing for business surrounding a tour.

Money

It's a difficult subject in any industry to talk about. Clarify your fee before you set off on the tour and NEVER speak of it again; Nobody wants to get the reputation of just being in it for the money! If you leave those talks at the door, it leaves more room to just enjoy the tour and focus on playing the best shows you can.

Dependant on the level of tour, your fees will likely vary from day to day; Often the rates are broken down as follows:

Show day

Rehearsal day

Off / Travel day

Some tours will just pay a flat day rate, however the majority will have a variance. *(As my touring schedule stands, I have 1 rate for Show days, and the other rate is flat for rehearsal, travel and off)*.

Regardless of this variance, you should always try to ensure you negotiate a rate *you* are comfortable with for every day you are away from home, as this is another day you cannot work for anyone else. It can feel precious, but it is both your **time** and your **skills** the artist is paying you for, so don't feel bad trying to secure payment for those 'off' days;

Don't get me wrong – If the artist is offering you a show rate you are happy with and there aren't too many 'off' days, take what I'm saying with a pinch of salt – don't jeopardise your booking for the sake of a few days. It's a different story however if you have 2 weeks worth of 'Off' or 'Travel' days.

There should also be a Per Diem (PD) payment every day which is essentially living expense money; This is generally perceived as lunch money before receiving your 'buyout' fee (same as a PD – cash up to a sum) or catering from the venue for dinner. If there is no gig on that day, your PD will likely be doubled.

Note: The PD is paid by the artist, the Buyout by the Promoter.

Some touring members opt to be frugal with their PD's and save them where possible, resorting to just eating Rider foods. Personally, I like to head out to local cafes or restaurants to get a feel for whichever city I may be in...*then again I was always the kid who spent his pocket money, instead of saving.*

It is important to note - The rates you set yourself and agree to can **affect your perceived image**. See Chapter 5, where Musical Directors discuss in more detail on how this can affect your bookabilty.

Remember why you are there.

Touring isn't just an excuse for that rock 'n' roll lifestyle...yes it is part and parcel of the experience, but you're there to build a business, whether your own or that of the artist who employs you. Even if you are employed on a session basis, you are carving a musical reputation with the other musicians on the gig, the management, the label, the agent, the crew...Be respectful to everyone you meet – you are an extension of the artist and everything you do will reflect in the image of both you and them.

The fans will look up to you and you will be treated as a member of that band! You might be the first guitarist that young fan has ever seen live...if you throw them to the crowd, it might be the first plectrum, drum stick or set list they have ever touched – These things could inspire them to start playing and that in itself is incredible...Be the role model you want to be remembered for!

Below is the image of a letter I received from a fan on our latest UK tour – I was so blown away by it, because I never knew until this moment that I was perceived as a role model in someone else's eyes; It just goes to show the energy you give during the time you are on stage, no matter how short, may alter the course of someone else's life for the better and give them a vision to aspire to!

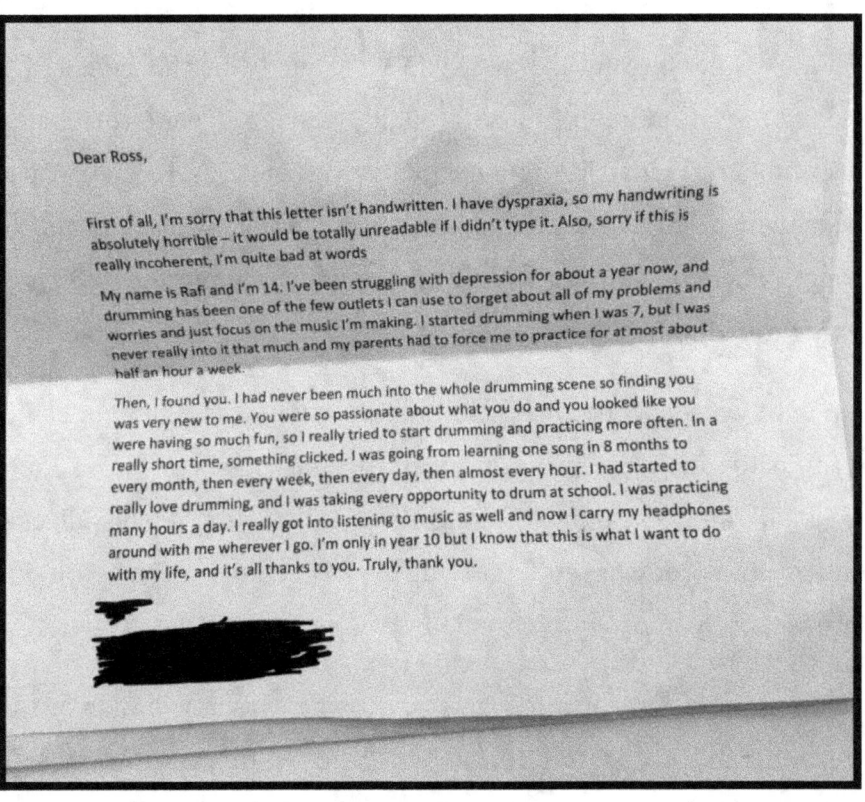

fan letter from dodie show @ The Roundhouse 2019

Remember why you started playing music in the first place

Think of who inspired you...

Think of the greatest shows you've ever seen...the songs that helped you through those tough teenage years of being heartbroken, being different, depressed or angry - I bet you can hear them in your head right now, can't you? I have my list of songs and I will forever idolise the bands that wrote them! This is why I found music.

Up until very recently, though, I'd lost sight of this. Sometimes it's easy to forget when you grind it out in this business for so long; You fall into a routine of long drives, load ins, sound checks, shows, pack downs and partying – it becomes menial on the surface, but you need to remind yourself it most definitely is not!

The moment that turned it around for me was my life in a full romantic and nostalgic circle; I was lucky enough to play a sold out show in the very same venue where I had seen my first ever gig - a sold out Jimmy Eat World concert, 15 years prior!

In an overwhelming sense of emotion, I came to the realisation that through all the personal and musical struggles, I *had* achieved my dreams – I was living them right then and there and continue to live them! I've now vowed to remind myself more often and I encourage you to do the same – *This* is why we play.

Screenshot taken from personal Instagram. (2019)

It reads:

"When I was younger I saw my first ever gig in this venue! It was Jimmy Eat World and I was completely in awe!...I stood on this second step on the left hand side and I could see everything. I watched the whole band, mesmerized, and I thought...THIS is what I want to do!

Tonight we headline to a sold out crowd and that's my drum riser I can see on the stage!

It's crazy how things can come full circle and it sometimes takes moments like these to realise you are living and making your own dreams come true. Thanks to everyone along the way who has and is continuing to make it all possible!"

Remember you are not indispensable

I've seen great musicians who have been fired off gigs because of their drinking habits or sloppy attitudes. You are an employee and just like any other business, if you are hindering progress or defacing the image, you will be let loose. There are a million other musicians waiting in the wings that would jump at a chance to take your spot. You've earned your right to be there, so don't give anyone a reason to take that away from you.

Be social and present

Don't always be on your phone or hiding away – the touring party will be your family and if you are open to it, you will share so many amazing memories for years to come with these people. Of course, everyone's personal needs are different so do what's best for you. Just don't miss out on all the wonderful opportunities by being a hermit!

Never think you are above a gig

Nobody is above paid work! As my mum always tells me - "As long as it's an honest pound!" Regardless of the environments you'll find yourself in (to an extent) always show that you care. You never know when your big gig may come to an end, so treat bread and butter gigs with respect – they will always be a staple diet for rent or mortgage payments in off season.

Try to avoid altercations

It's easy to get wound up when you are in such close proximity with others for long periods of time and working in high pressure environments. Find a way of decompressing if you are stressed and don't vent your frustrations on others.

We play a game called 'Tour Court' - Essentially it is a bit like Parliament where both positive and negative issues can be raised in a light hearted manner and discussed with the touring party – the group will then decide if it is 'fine worthy' and punishable by wrist slaps, or, if you have done something good for the team, rewarded with a round of applause. We keep a running tally and award a 'legend' and 'dick' of tour at the end of the run in a ceremonial fashion. The most coveted award is controversially the 'dick' trophy...of which I have a few!

This process serves in clearing the air and avoids any bitchiness or frustrations that may have manifested into bigger problems further down the line.

Know your chain of command

Ever been at a gig and seen a load of people wondering around and not really know what they do? They are probably a lot more important than you think!

In a session capacity, everyone works for the artist.

On a tour, the next in command is likely to be the **Tour Manager** or **Production Manager**. The artist's day-to-day **manager** may also make an appearance from time to time, but for all things non-musical and tour related your first port of call should be the TM.

If you have any worries music related, your first port of call is likely the **Musical Director**, who will (9 times out of 10) be the band leader. If they need to then delegate your issues elsewhere, then so be it. (Curious what a Musical Director does? – jump to chapter 5)

Other people who will be around on tour or likely to show up will be:

The Promoter & Rep: These are the people who run the shows; The bigger the promoter, the more people you are likely to encounter. Promoters are essentially middle men between venues and booking agents and will negotiate with the booking agent about ticket splits or fees. The promoter or their rep will be responsible for all things practical on the show day on and off stage and ensuring the smooth running of the show. Eg. Purchasing and setting up the band's rider, towels for showering, food buyouts, sticking to soundcheck times and running order etc.

Booking Agent: The booking agent will work for the artist and be responsible for booking and routing the tour. They will be responsible for negotiating the best deal for the artist, working closely with the promoter to ensure the smooth running of the entire live proceedings. Having an agent will allow you to play bigger and better shows, take the responsibility off your shoulders allowing you to focus on the gig itself. They may also be able to secure you good support slots if they work for other bigger or prominent artists.

Merchandise Manager: Often bands will tour with their own merch person responsible for overseeing any hired hands who may be working on the show. They will be responsible for all merch money generated, taking it to the bank, and ensuring reports and stocks are accurate. This is a big job, as merchandise is where tours can make the majority of their income.

Publisher: The band or artist's publishers may turn up – These are the people who are responsible for the commercial exploitation of the artist's musical works. They will be responsible for collecting all royalty generated income and search to find placement opportunities for the band or artist, including sync to TV, Film, Advertising and Gaming.

Label: If the artist is signed to an independent or major label, there will likely be a big team behind them, including A&R's, Marketing, PR etc. All of these people can potentially be seen at shows. The most common would be the A&R who is part of the division responsible for talent scouting and the artistic and creative development of the artist.

Crew: Needless to say you should know your touring/gigging crew already, however, the different departments on the road will likely include **Front of House** (what the audience hears), **Monitors** (what you hear), **Lighting & SFX** and **Backline Techs** (the guys who look after the instruments, instrument changes, tuning guitars, setting up mic placements, loading in & out etc).

There will also be **local crew** in most venues – these guys will be helping with load in / load out, so be nice or they may throw your gear around...well, more than they do already! On bigger production shows, there may be carpenters, electricians, riggers, stylists etc.

Venue Manager / Security / Bar Staff: Self explanatory

Bus Driver: Treat him/her with respect – they will be your best mate on a tour and responsible for your safety and comfort.

Support Acts. Curious how to get a support slot? See chapter 7.

It is important to differentiate between these different roles, as everyone will be busy and stressed enough within their own fields to burden them with something not really in their remit.

If you do all of these things, you will gain the respect of the team whose links will span far into the music industry and with them so will your name. Your reputation in this game is your worth...and therefore **your business and your product.**

Health

"Your health is your wealth"

There's no beating around the bush – touring is not the healthiest way to live, but there are ways to make sure you try and stay on top of your game.

Diet

*"You can't expect to look like a million bucks
if you eat from the dollar menu"*

With the introduction of Netflix, there has come a vast array of health and wellbeing documentaries stating the importance of diet – of course, this is old news, but at least the knowledge of how diet can impact your life for the better or worse is now becoming a widespread phenomenon.

We all know the famous adage - *"You are what you eat"*

How are you supposed to deliver night on night if your body is running on fumes? Gone are the days of rockstars surviving on nothing but cocaine, fags and whisky...I mean, sure, these elements all still exist depending on what circles you run in, but the modern day image of music and diet are changing. Riders these days are packed with tons of healthy items and alternatives to meat, dairy and sugar etc.

Performing is an athletic activity, so we need to ensure we are giving our bodies the best input for maximum output. We require hydration and stamina, so be sure to drink a load of water throughout the day;

Dr. Timothy Jameson states:

> *"Cellular and muscular function is severely limited when dehydration is present. It is estimated that muscles lose 30% of their contractile ability when dehydrated."*

He goes on to tell us our body has no way of telling us when we are dehydrated – we actually feel thirsty long after dehydration begins. If you exert a lot of energy and sweat during your performance you may need up to 12 glasses of water the days before and after your gig to adequately recuperate.

Food

It sounds obvious, but try to eat well on the road! It's so easy to get distracted by all the sugary sweets and drinks laid out on your rider or be consumed by the idea of a late night MacDonald's when you pull into a service station, but it's important to avoid caving to these pressures too often or the body will just crash (...and put on a load of weight).

Natural snacks, such as nuts, seeds, berries, beans, fruits, vegetables etc. are a much better choice over caffeine and sugary treats which drastically affect your blood and insulin levels. Jesse Sterling Harrison for Sonicbids Blog states:

> *"Sugary sweets are metabolised almost immediately and force your body to crash as soon as the sugar burns away!"*

It can be okay for a short burst of energy, but once the insulin removes the sugar from the body you will crash and burn!

A better option for a slow release of steady energy needed for an entire show or a recording session is a good balance of protein and carbohydrates; This could be something as simple as hummus or bean dips, to bananas and different types of nut butters. **Whole grains** (*oats, brown rice & bread etc*), **fatty acids** (*avocados & nuts*) and **omega 3's** (*fish or supplements*) are also advisable, along with green leafy vegetables.

Dr. Timothy Jameson goes on to state:

"The worst thing you can do is go more than three or four hours without food while recording (or performing) music. Your mind will not last because of lowered blood sugar levels due to the high demands of concentration during your performance. This will lead to irritation, tendencies towards anger and frustration, and poor playing ability."

Vitamins

When it is advisable to try and get all of your dietary requirements from natural food sources, we all know it's not always possible. Health shops are becoming more of a high street trend, so it's good practice to stock up on essentials if you are headed out on a long run...or even just after better well being here at home. Given that our job is physical, we want our bodies to be well oiled machines that function with longevity and sustainability – vitamins are key, regardless of how you get them...just make sure you do!

Vitamin C will always be your best friend on a tour and is a rider essential – Once you get sick on a tour, it's difficult to overcome! Study researcher Mark Moyad (MD, MPH) from the University of Michigan explains:

"Vitamin C has received a great deal of attention (over the last 10 years), and with good reason. Higher blood levels of vitamin C may be the ideal nutrition marker for overall health."

The vitamin is an essential nutrient for our bodies and promotes well being by supporting our immune system, maintaining healthy bones and teeth, creating collagen (the most abundant protein in our bodies that comprises ligaments, muscles and skin) and efficiency of wound healing to name but a few of it's benefits.

Other advisable supplements for general wellbeing include a good multivitamin, green super foods and omega 3's.

Green super foods lower the acidity of the body and neutralise pH levels to a more optimum level. The body thrives in a more alkaline state, however modern diets (including alcohol consumption) are contributing to more acidity, creating problems such as an increased risk of cancer, weight gain, poor organ function and digestion and lowered energy levels.

Omega 3's are essential fatty acids often found in fish oils. They contribute to brain health (sometimes helping depression or mood swings) and are anti-inflammatory, bringing benefits to your joints, muscles, gut and skin.

Keep it interesting!

On our rider, we allow each person on the tour to choose one item they would like to see – it makes for some interesting combinations, especially in foreign locations, but always keeps it fresh. We also have a number of vegetarians on our team which encourages everyone else to think about their food choices.

On another tour, we asked for one surprise local edible and/or local beers or spirit on each gig. This can make you look forward to your rider and stop it becoming too predictable and monotonous.

(Touring Hack – Buy a George Foreman grill – it will transform your rider foods!)

Alcohol

Alcohol is one of those tour rider items which seems near impossible to avoid; Some members will choose to try and have a dry tour, but from experience it's not for the faint hearted, given the build up of adrenaline, emotions and celebrations surrounding a successful show, night after night. This and the fact it is just. always. there!

(Note: Many touring bands will opt to have a dry tour with no alcohol on their rider – I'm yet to experience this!)

It does become very easy to abuse and dangerous routines are never too far away, especially if you are touring for long periods of time.

We all know of the famous musicians who have succumb to a life...and sadly, death, of substance and alcohol abuse; Elvis Presley, Janis Joplin, Jimi Hendrix, Kurt Cobain, Amy Winehouse to name a few.

But why does it become so difficult to tolerate and why do so many turn to it?

Instability – Making a living from music is a choice not for the faint hearted. Lacking the stability of a guaranteed wage and the high and low swings of a life on tour requires a certain personality type. It can become easy to abuse alcohol in both of these instances, whether highs during celebration and success, or lows to combat depression, boredom, worry or uncertainty.

Availability – As mentioned above; It is always there. Gigs are fun events, where people come to have a good time, lower their inhibitions and let themselves live for the night; Now imagine doing this 150+ times a year – Late nights and free drinks can lead to habits, and in some cases, addiction.

Musicians can often fall into the following category: *Egomaniacs with low self esteem*; translated – they want everyone to love them, but they hate themselves. This is also the same category alcoholics fall into. If you are reading this, I can guarantee you, or someone you know identifies as this personality type.

Don't get me wrong, I'm not condemning alcohol; In fact it is the lifeblood of many music venues, which without would struggle to support live music! It is not the substance that is bad, it's the abuse. If you can control it, it is a great tool to be enjoyed.

I'm not here to preach – I come from a Scottish culture that love a good 'bevvie' and I'm no different.

All I would say is:

Tours are long. Remember it is a marathon, not a sprint. If you run yourself in to the ground, it will be hard to recuperate.

Try to pick your moments to have big nights out - The best nights to choose are "Roadie Friday's" (*Nights where you will have no show the day after*).

You can still have a good few drinks on a show night, but with all the scheduling for the following day it is simply not worth the pain to go too big...and of course the risk of not performing to the best of your ability; This will just ruin your enjoyment of an otherwise great show, which could also jeopardise your job & reputation.

Singers, be careful with drinking too much before a show – Alcohol targets small muscle groups such as vocal chords which can reduce control.

If you are on a show with a decent rider you could have multiple bottles of many different spirits, so pick your tour drink wisely; My current tipple is a Tequila & Tonic – *...I know, I know!*

Otherwise known as a 'Tectonic', it was introduced to me by a seasoned touring friend (*and FOH engineer of the year 2018 I might add*) Mr. Mike Woodhouse. His reasoning being - it's super clean and lessens the hangover. As dubious as I was, there is some science behind this;

Emily Han, author of Wild Drinks and Cocktails states *"blanco tequila contains a lower level of congeners than dark spirits and red wine. Congeners are substances like acetone and tannins that are produced during fermentation and ageing, and studies show they may worsen hangovers."*

...And with only 98 calories (roughly) a shot it will also stop you piling on the pounds, unlike the old trusty can of beer.

Sleep

"Sleep is the golden chain that ties health and our bodies together"

Thomas Dekker

We spend close to a third of our lives asleep – it is essential for survival and well being. It has an affect on both physical and mental health and our quality of life.

The National Heart Lung and Blood Institute explains:

"The way you feel when you're awake depends in part what happens while you're sleeping. Sleep helps your brain work properly, forming new pathways to help learn and remember information, supporting heathy brain function and maintaining your physical health."

Your immune system relies on sleep to stay healthy. A lack of it can result in getting sick and on a tour, this is the last thing you want!

"Ongoing sleep deficiency can change the way in which your immune system responds. For example, if you're sleep deficient, you may have trouble fighting common infections."

It goes on to state that deprivation may alter problem solving, creativity, controlling your emotions and behaviour and the ability to cope with change. It is also linked to suicide and depression.

All of these factors would undoubtedly have an impact on your playing and mental state, especially given all the other pressures of touring, so it's advisable to try and get at least 7 hours sleep at night.

Sleeping on a tour bus isn't for everyone; some find it hard with the motion of the bus or the bumps in the road. Personally, I feel like I sleep better on a bus than I do in my own bed at home!

Fitness

With the heavy workloads that you may encounter on tour and irregular sleeping patterns it's not always easy to motivate yourself to stay fit. Some of the more sensible members of touring parties manage to get in a healthy routine...often going to bed at a reasonable hour and getting up early for exercise; This can be a nice way to see a city that you've never been to before the work day starts (fortunately for the musicians, this is often later than the crew who are the unsung heroes of any tour).

Gyms are never too far away in all the big cities if you are on a bus tour, and if your TM is that way inclined on a splitter tour, hotels often will have a fitness centre; You may even be fortunate enough to land a big tour which tours it's own gym or personal trainers, but that's a very small percentage. On one US tour we decided to buy some weights and a bench on Craigslist for $100 which we toured for 4 weeks and then re-sold before our last show...for a profit I might add.

Fun team sports activities are also a good idea to motivate those lazier members; 5 aside football, basketball...even a game of catch. It's also good form to include other acts on the tour as a good way to socialise and get to know each other – this is also a great networking opportunity and will leave a much stronger lasting memory than being just 'that guy from that band'.

In Europe & the US it's easy to download apps to rent bikes and scooters which is again another nice way to see the cities. (*Lime is a good one*).

It is important to stay fit as a musician – people are coming to see you perform at your best and you don't want to give them a sub par show; Performing is an athletic ability and just like any sport you need to keep in shape for the job you are doing. Both regular fitness and warm ups are important to prevent injuries occurring, but also to keep your mental faculties strong. Exercising improves your mood, your cognitive function and concentration. It will also allow you to have better endurance for those headline sets of 1-2 hours.

Warm ups don't have to be vigorous; From a drummer's perspective – do some singles, doubles, different sticking patterns and some simple stretching at least. I used to be terrible for it and never warmed up, but having sorted out my pre-show routine in the last few years, it really does loosen you up and you will perform better! Guitarists, do some scales...vocalists, do some breathing exercises, the lip buzz or the siren (*a real thing*). There are tons of warm up videos for each instrument on YouTube, so just pick one that works for you that you enjoy.

Mental Health

"Writing a song has never made me unhappy...
It's the industry, it's the game"

Lauren Aquilina

Musical mental health is somewhat of a new discussion, but is one of the most prevalent issues; Most touring musicians will tell you – it is a roller-coaster of emotions and you may not always know why you are feeling a certain way, so it is good practice to talk honestly with your bandmates about any issues that may be niggling you.

You may have problems at home, you may be home-sick, you might be stressed about a difficult part you have to play or something in the show not working correctly...You might suffer with terrible nerves or anxiety...or just having one of those days. This goes hand in hand with our physical health section above, as of course any hangovers, unhealthy diets or lack of sleep will add to the pressures of whatever you are dealing with.

One common topic of discussion (which is benefited by this link between fitness and positive brain function discussed above) is that of lowering anxiety within performers. One study, shown at https://bit.ly/2R7luvo, discusses how regular aerobic activity can in fact lower both generalised anxiety and anxiety sensitivity.

But what is anxiety sensitivity, I hear you ask?

Well, we know generalised anxiety is the normal human response in pressure situations – increased heart rate, butterflies or gut wrenching feelings in our stomach, combined with faster breathing and a heightened sense of alertness. Essentially, this is the feeling you get before you walk on stage.

But what happens when the anxiety doesn't stop there? Do you ever find yourself over-thinking about the anxiety itself...snowballing every little detail until you're a nervous wreck who's convinced the audience will hate you, resulting in a loss of job, home and total self worth? This seems a bit drastic, but this train of thought has been identified as 'anxiety sensitivity'; Essentially an anxiety about anxiety...or as sixteenth century philosophical essayist Michel de Montaigne wrote "The thing I fear the most is fear".

Harvard Medical School state:

"Anxiety sensitivity is a tendency to misinterpret the sensations that accompany anxiety — irregular breathing, heart palpitations, trembling, flushing, sweating, stomach rumbling — as indications of imminent physical danger or serious illness ("I'm going to have a heart attack;" or "I'm going to faint"), loss of control ("I can't concentrate — I'm going crazy!"), or humiliating social rejection ("Everyone will notice that I'm trembling")."

Understanding anxiety sensitivity may make it easier to understand the feelings you are experiencing and stop the downward spiral you may find yourself in - Of course this is easier said than done, but awareness is surely the first step!

On a recent European Tour I suffered my own version of anxiety sensitivity; *(excerpt taken from blog)*

"I've always been one for giving it my all on a gig and leaving it all out there on stage...never really over thinking my parts and just playing from the heart; It's always done me well and I thrive in that live environment.

I was playing a solo in the final song of the set, when I suddenly became very aware of myself – completely out of nowhere, playing a song I've played hundreds of times to tens of thousands of people. I was over analysing my movements, technique, ideas etc. as I was performing – a real out of body experience. I essentially gave myself a complex there and then about something that was never a problem to begin with.

I came off stage feeling a bit rubbish and I felt I had to talk to the band about it and apologised for my sloppy playing...guess what? Nobody had noticed anything out of place or off about my performance. Spoke to the fans who told me they loved that section of the song...it was so much worse in my own head than in the reality of the moment."

Taken from @rosscraib Instagram blog

I had felt that by messing up in a public space, people would think less of me; You get so used to people being critical of music that you think if you put even the smallest foot wrong, you will be outed.

It turns out these feelings are a lot more common than you think!

"When a musician develops a heightened fear of criticism, the result can vary from profound feelings of anxiety to depression. I honestly believed that every time I went on stage, every single

person in the room was an expert in music and was critiquing every note." - Help Musicians UK

Help Musicians, a UK run charity, recently performed a study into the mental health of 2,000+ self-selected musicians across the industry; They found that **more than 70% had experienced panic attacks and anxiety, with close to 70% having experienced depression.**

"Preliminary findings suggested that while artists find solace in the production of music, working in the music industry might indeed be making musicians sick, or at least contributing to their levels of mental ill-health"

These were based on a number of factors such as poor working conditions (sustainability, inability to plan a future, exhaustion), a lack of recognition for one's work, physical impacts and injuries and being a woman in the industry etc.

Given that the majority of musicians are highly self-critical and perfectionistic, in an industry that requires a lot of self-belief, it is easy for confidence to be knocked in an environment of constant critical feedback. Careers in music are unpredictable and with music and success being the biggest definer in a musician's sense of self, it can be difficult to know who you truly are, thus affecting your happiness.

We therefore have to try and find methods of detracting or disengaging from these negative feelings to allow ourselves a better mental health. Awareness and physical wellbeing is key, as is knowing that you're not alone...but what else can we do?

I recently read an interesting blog post from an acquaintance of mine, Sam Skirrow, who I met in Austria whilst he was on tour playing bass for Clean Bandit. His post was titled **"You are not your business"** and it focussed on the separation between you as a business and you as *you* in an attempt to gain better mental health!

I found it interesting because he is completely correct; It is very easy to blur the lines. If you get fired from a gig, or a tour gets pulled or you get told not to *"play like that"*, it can feel like a personal attack – you take it personally...but it isn't personal – It's business. More often than not it's down to things that fall outside of your control, such as budget cuts or not being the right fit for a project – these are based on your *product* and not based on you as a person.

Sam writes:

"Thinking like this gives me a better headspace. I feel a sense of space and clarity in how to make business moves – it may even feel like my business is failing (and it often does), but, I don't feel like I am failing."

Ross with Clean Bandit & Sam Skirrow, Anne Marie & Bry @ Frequency Festival (2017)

Understand how your brain works

Another great post I read by Noa Kageyama PH.D. from the 'Bulletproof Musician' was that of turning performance anxiety into an asset instead of a liability, using adrenaline as power to enhance creative freedom and confidence.

In order to achieve this, amongst other remedies and strategies, we must first understand why our brain reacts in the way it does in a stressed state;

> *"Our brains can be thought of as being comprised of two basic regions – the left hemisphere and the right hemisphere. Admittedly, it is an oversimplification, but this is a very helpful model when it comes to understanding optimal mental states for performance.*

Left brain thinking is associated with words, numbers, logic, analysis, criticism, rules, details, planning, and judgment. Conversely, right brain thinking is associated with sounds, images, patterns, kinaesthetic or sensory input, emotions, the "big picture," free association, and creativity."

Given that the left brain is more conducive to logic and planning, you'd assume it would be the hemisphere we use the most when practicing, allowing the right brain to control our emotions for inspired and creative performances in live scenarios. Unfortunately, the inverse is what actually happens; In rehearsal rooms we often play with freedom in a somewhat unconscious state repeating phrases and techniques.

"However, as soon as we walk onstage, we tend to get flooded by left brain over-analytical thinking, criticism, excessive planning, and so on, which only serves to lead to a pre-occupation with technical details and an inability to play as freely and automatically as we are capable"

- Noa Kageyama

Once again, understanding why we feel anxious in performance situations is the first step on the road to combating those fears and anxieties; The remedies that suit every individual can then follow. In this instance, Kageyama references a technique called 'Centering' – a term coined by sports psychologists in the 70's, it is a highly effective means of channelling nerves productively and directing focus in extreme situations. To read more in detail about how to 'centre' yourself, visit bulletproofmusician.com!

Pre Stage Routines

A pre stage routine is good way to get in the zone for a performance...it gives you that sense of regularity and excitement that something great is about to happen in a world where nothing on the surface is *that* normal.

Our crew has a pre stage routine that starts around 30 minutes prior to stage time; We pour a drink and sing and dance to old pop-punk songs from the 00's...Avril Lavigne, Miley Cyrus, Paramore etc. We get glitter put on our faces by the artist to match her aesthetic. This leads up to the most ridiculous gospel song you've ever heard – we're not a religious bunch, but 'Desire' by Kierra Sheard has become our jam, with 3 key changes, band stabs, gospel fills & runs and crying vocalists...it truly is a roller coaster and is our final song before we walk to stage.

When we reach the side of the stage we play a game called 'Zimmy Zimmy' - a team warm up where each member receives a number and has to pass the 'go' onto another number in the circle until someone sends it back to home ('Zimmy');

For example "1,1,3,3.....3,3,5,5...5,5,2,2...2,2,Zimmy,Zimmy...and so on"

The game gets faster and faster every time it gets passed back to 'Zimmy' until someone drops the ball. This gets us pumped before walking on upon light drop.

Routines like these are positive for the mental health of not only individuals on a tour, but the group. It is good team building and helps you get your brain in gear before the walk on.

Photo Credit: Mathew Parri Thomas
'Zimmy Zimmy' Pre Stage Routine @ The Roundhouse 2019

Burnout

Burnout can occur in any industry, but in ours it is sadly very common. As per anxiety and depression, burnout too is a mental health disorder triggered by excessive and prolonged stress – in some cases, anxiety and depression may even be the cause or contributing factor.

Burnout is described by Help Guide as:

"...a state of emotional, physical, and mental exhaustion. It occurs when you feel overwhelmed, emotionally drained, and unable to meet constant demands. As the stress continues, you begin to lose the interest and motivation that led you to take on a certain role in the first place. Burnout reduces productivity and saps your energy, leaving you feeling increasingly helpless, hopeless, cynical, and resentful. Eventually, you may feel like you have nothing more to give."

What causes burnout in musicians and how to avoid it?

The number one (*at least in my life and that of some of my close friends*) has always been **monetary stability and regularity**. Fortunately, I now have the ability to survive as a full time musician, thanks to many of the things I've written about in this very book, however, I have experienced burnout, anxiety and depression in the past and know that it is a dark hole full of spiralling negativity and questioning life choices. The best advice I could give is to have enough alternative forms of income to help alleviate some of those financial pressures until you can sustain it full time. Pick time flexible jobs that you'd be happy to leave in an instant or with bosses who understand the sector you are trying to succeed in.

On the flip side to this, as I mentioned in my 'Attitude' section; Remember why you started playing music in the first place! Some people can get so **caught up in the money**, they forget why they started playing music in the first place. I know we are trying to be successful and make money from our passion...but don't lose sight of that passion! It's one of the quickest paths on the road to resentment, and ultimately burnout.

Not advancing in your career. Again, I've been there! From experience, it's very easy to blame everyone but yourself for being stuck in a rut. Sometimes you have to take a step back to see the bigger picture - Maybe it requires a different tact. The work isn't magically going to fall from the sky straight into your lap...sure, things happen and phone calls will (from time to time) come out of the blue, but not if you don't put yourself in the right position. Create the opportunities for yourself! (More on this in Chapter 5! Networking & Getting the Gig)

Not enough time for family or friends. Ensure that you allow yourself downtime. It's very easy to get caught up in, and sometimes obsessed with, musical projects or ideas. We're musicians – we LIVE music...but try to live it well! Make time for your partner and family and give them support. They need it just as much as you! Heads up – Don't talk about music all the time or you'll bore the life out of them!

Signs you may be heading towards burnout

Lack of focus. Your brain might be flooded with a million different tasks and rather than checking off your to-do list one by one, you jump from pillar to post trying to spin all the metaphorical plates at once. This is super unproductive and a sign that you are nearing burnout. Being present and engaged may also be a symptom; If you are struggling to hold conversations with family or friends without being able to switch off, this is a sign,; The same can be said with the inability to switch off at night time, which may manifest itself in insomnia.

Procrastination. Rather than cracking on and getting stuff done (combined with your lack of focus) you may decide to avoid the problems and work altogether. Sometimes it's easier just to put Netflix on or mind-numbingly scroll through Facebook and Instagram. Some people resort to alcohol as an escapism, but when it's to avoid the thing that's supposed to bring you joy, and if your career - income, changes must be made to deter from this negative coping mechanism.

The way you feel about your project and how you talk about it with others. Ever get asked that generic music question: "Hey how's everything going? Still doing your project?" and brush it off with a vague answer that projects success, even though inside you're dying with feelings of uncertainty, guilty and worry? This is a sign. If you are not excited about your project any more and feel like you have to lie to feel accepted, ask yourself why.

In this situation it is easy to **vent your frustrations on others**; You may make excuses or look to place blame elsewhere. Resentment of other people's success is an issue and a really negative place to be. Instead of seeing the negatives in others, try to pinpoint their successes and replicate them for your own project. The world doesn't hate you or your project...you may have just hit the wall and need a new tact or lease of life. Take a step back and evaluate, rather than driving yourself (and your reputation if you get caught bitching) into the ground.

Conclusion

To truly avoid burnout and for a healthier brain, it is important to step back and see your life as a bigger picture; Make sure everything doesn't revolve around music. If it does, your life is just one dimensional...and instead of burning out at your job, you are essentially just burning out at life.

Have hobbies, play sports, go on holidays, see the world, make new friends, learn new languages...whatever it is, to maximise your enjoyment and musical potential, you must detract temporarily from the music itself.

How to combat bad mental health on tour - Summary

Know that you're not alone! 70% of musicians suffer from anxiety and depression from a wide range of factors.

Understand that anxiety sensitivity may be making you feel worse in a gigging scenario, but try to see it for what it is to combat it.

Understand your brain is only doing what is natural! Go with it and try to find remedies that work for you!

If you feel yourself getting burned out, take a step back and try to live a little outside of music. It will feel refreshing. Nobody wants to work with a tired, grumpy, burnt out musician.

All of the aforementioned chapters contribute to mental health on the road – Diet, Fitness & Sleep! It's your choice whether these are positive or negative. Just remember for good output, we need good input.

Your support network is key – always pick others up when they feel down and they will do the same for you! Believe in yourself and your abilities, as you will always be your own worst critic. Try and see yourself the way others see you and just enjoy the on stage experience. It's live music after all and no 2 shows are identical...there in lies the beauty.

Try to see the separation between you and your product and be aware people aren't watching a show to critique you – they are there to have a good time.

Remember you are on tour for a reason; you've earned it – as a session player an artist has put their faith in you and you are there on merit. They trust you, so you have to trust yourself.

Getting the gig & Networking

The age old question – "How do you get the gig?" Truth be told, there is no correct way or golden bullet to this! However, there is a word that will help in your journey – *Networking*!

What is networking?

Networking is essentially growing your professional contact base by creating meaningful relationships, best achieved by socialising and just being yourself.

I remember my first day at music school where we got told this would be the "greatest tool in your arsenal" – I couldn't get my head around where to even begin. Fast forward 10 years, it's in fact very simple – be a good person and chat to others; Go to events (gigs, jams, parties, trade shows etc.) and be current in people's minds.

Now, I'm not saying go to these gatherings to 'fish' for work – this will be very obvious and likely turn people off giving you any potential future work! What I mean is, just go out, be present and let your personality shine; Music in itself is about personality, so you have to be able to get yours across in social settings.

Conversation is key!

This doesn't have to be all about music! Chat about anything...sport, movies, politics, relationships etc. If I'm honest, I'd rather have a meaningful conversation about general *stuff* than talk about what drum heads I use or how many plies of maple my snare drum has! This can be said for the majority of professional musicians and will leave people with a stronger lasting memory of your personality for the next time you meet.

And meet again you shall...

What you will come to realise very quickly is that music is in fact a very small 'network' of people with similar faces appearing at many different events – rather than 5 degrees of separation, it's more like 1 or 2 at most, so try to be upbeat and a fun person to be around! Word spreads quickly in musical circles and the last thing you want is a negative reputation.

In my experience most, if not all of my biggest gigs have come from friends or word of mouth. Less so from auditions, however, these can still be a viable route if the opportunities arise.

A good friend of mine and Musical Director, Sam Kennedy, states that most of his musical successes in the beginning came from A&R'ing the artists he wanted to work with himself:

*"Don't write to all the MD's because we have millions of people asking us for gigs. The most successful way of being a session musician or an MD is having a good ability to **A&R** the artists you want to work for.*

*In the beginning for me, people like **Jess Glynne, Foxes, John Newman**...all people I was fortunate to work with, (MD'ing, recording, producing or writing) were all voices that I had just gone out and found. I'd never written to an MD, Agent or Booker – I had just searched for the best talent I could find and hit them up to work together. This way it will become your gig and will be your best ticket into the industry. MD's or agents will then see you on stage with these artists or you will end up meeting each other at a gig and your details will be exchanged."*

Be brutal when deciding who to invest your time with if you go this route; Don't waste your time on a project if they have a great voice, but poor songs – it's likely not going to go anywhere. Invest your time wisely – search Facebook, Instagram, Youtube, go to open mic nights, check out 'Mahognay' or 'Balcony TV' etc. and try to find artists who need what you offer (piano, guitar, drums, writing). It's the best place to start and a far more proactive way of getting gigs versus spending 5 hours on your laptop sending profile pictures of yourself to agents, who probably have that 100 times a day.

The road to the biggest gig of my career:

I had a quiet Christmas one year, so in true pioneering fashion, I decided to go in search of the work myself; I scoured the internet looking at 'drummer wanted' ads and eventually stumbled on a singer with a great voice and some lovely songs.

I approached her with my then reasonable CV and told her I could put a band together for her. There wasn't a lot of money in it, but I decided to take a punt anyway just for the love of the music and, well…you just never know where it might take you.

I took to Facebook in search of some musicians and due to the low paying nature of this gig didn't have too many responses. One chap popped up – his name was Pete; It emerged we had worked for the same Major Label artist, Martin Luke Brown, but just at different times in our career; (We had in fact met through said artist at a Wetherspoons once upon a time, which began our online friendship, however, this was our only encounter.)

I gave Pete a call and explained all the info on the gig – He liked the vibe of the project and like me, decided to take a punt on it – Until now, we had never played together; Of course this requires trust, but trust is built on the network in which you have mutual friends – I trusted them, so in turn, I trusted Pete. Never did I know where this one gesture would lead us both within 4 years.

We performed together a handful of times, recording an EP for this artist, but nothing really came of it. Fortunately though, a similar scenario had arisen where Pete had been asked to look after another emerging artist; Because I was fresh in his memory and we'd had a good time working together, he offered me the gig and our working relationship grew even stronger.

We played one show together and I remember it being KILLER...one of the best I've played – we still talk about it to this day, in fact! During load out Pete told me he was very excited about another artist he had just heard from – her name was dodie; A singer-songwriter superstar in the making who had amassed millions of fans from her Youtube content.

She needed a band for a tour and Pete had been asked to MD the band; Unfortunately for me, another mutual friend of ours was first in line for the throne, however there were some clashes in his diary – as it emerged he had just taken on a touring theatre show for the next year. My phone rang the next week and the rest, as they say, is history! I joined the band in December 2016 and have never looked back!

Pete and I have since toured the world 7 times together with dodie and performed on her Top 5 UK Official Album, 'Human'...And it all stemmed from that one little Facebook post all these years ago and a couple of beers in Wetherspoons; This, in my eyes, was the perfect example of networking combined with musicianship paying off.

Photo credit: Stevie Kyle
Pete Daynes & I backstage at The Barrowlands, Glasgow 2019

Photo Credit: Kyle Jones
dodie – Human EP, which charted at No.5 on The UK Official Album Chart

Networking On Tour

On tour there are a vast amount of learning resources at your fingertips. Keep your eyes and ears open and you will become a better professional!

Watch how others work; If there are a few bands on tour with you...check out what you counterpart is doing, how they play, how they interact. Learn from their set up – is there anything you could incorporate into your own playing?

Use your surroundings as an education. See who is working with whom and learn their personalities - Some of my best touring friends aren't even band members. It's easy sometimes to go a whole tour without really getting to know certain crew members, so make the effort.

Use common sense - Don't make a nuisance of yourself by getting in the way, but you won't do much harm by being around with a smiley face. Offer cups of tea or coffee every now and again; It will go a long way – these are the guys behind the scenes who make you look and sound great.

Musical Directors

What is a Musical Director?

A Musical Director is the person responsible for the musical aspects of a performance. They will likely source the musicians, arrange and coordinate the show and lead rehearsals to ensure everything is ready for the tour, allowing the artist to focus on the performance.

They will have an in depth knowledge of technical playback softwares, such as Ableton, MIDI controllers etc. and all the programming that goes with it. As such, they will need a good grasp on all the hardware required and often be competent multi-instrumentalists to know what is playable live and what will need to go on 'track' (if applicable).

Their job is to replicate, to the best of their ability, the sound recordings of the artist in a live environment and bring it to life. It can be a stressful job, but is a very employable attribute to add to your CV.

In their own words:

"An MD's role varies from project to project. In a sense, the title of 'Musical Director' covers such a vast amount of responsibilities depending on who or what you're working for – that covering the entire position across all musical projects, from orchestras to musicals to choir leaders to pop artists would require an entire book on it's own. For this case, we'll focus on an MD's role from a pop music standpoint.

An MD's primary role is to understand the artist's musical vision and direction, and translate that into a live music environment. This in itself means that the working relationship between an artist and MD has to be a very close one, as it is their expertise in technology, arrangement and musician contacts that can help realise this vision. It's a two way street though, as the MD should also have a very strong understanding of the music, not just on an instrumental level, but lyrically too. This will help build trust and understanding between the two parties and as such, a mould for a setlist/show should present itself relatively easily." **- Pete Daynes (dodie, Orla Gartland)**

"The long and short of it: The MD is responsible for all elements of a live show, from who is appearing on stage, to what songs ultimately are being played and how they are being played...even down to who the Front of House sound engineer is going to be. All the elements that go around this combine to make for a fairly hefty job – there are a lot of moving parts." **- Anon**

What do Musical Director's look for in Musicians?

This is a vast question, so I decided to bring in some external MD's to help answer in their own words what attributes they look for in the musicians they employ. Due to the honest nature of this section, I've opted to keep some of the contributors anonymous to protect identities, as they are some of the most respected in the UK industry.

It is also important to note - these are opinions from a range of different people and they will vary and likely contradict each other in some way as one size does not fit all when it comes to music!

The long and short of it...There are a lot of moving parts!

"It's important to understand this, simply because when you're looking at booking a band or musicians, you are essentially *not* going to be interested in anybody who would cause more stress or more work. I've booked people in the past who have sent me emails, texts or calls asking if their tube fare is going to be covered, or they tell me they can't get on the tube with their guitar for fear of it being damaged and therefore wanting me to find out if there is a budget for a taxi to the rehearsal; These are fairly inexperienced questions, but it puts me in a position where I think "I can't be dealing with this – I just need you to know your parts, turn up on time, play them well and go home – It really is that cut and dry to be honest." - **Anon**

Be a good player

"When you have that much responsibility for a show you don't have time really to be worrying about the tiny details you would expect a session musician to have covered. So really you are looking for a session musician who obviously needs to be a good player – that's a given. But by 'good' player, I don't mean Joe Satriani or Mike Portnoy! When you're talking about a good session player, you are talking about somebody who can perform proficiently; So for drummers, that is ability to play to a click track. For a guitarist, someone who has a very reliable sound and feel and can just play the parts as they appear on the record;

I think that's a very good rule for any session musician – PLAY WHAT'S THERE on the record; Do not play anything else! I'm not interested in guitar solos, gospel drum chops, bass fill licks – Just play what's on the record and what the MD sends you on the stems! (If you work with a well organised MD they will probably send you these for the parts they want you to play. Stems are essentially isolated tracks. i.e. If you are a piano or keys player, it can often be confusing as to which parts you might be playing on a pop record – there might be synths, strings, pianos, organs...all sorts, so the MD will have decided ahead of time what parts he wants you to play.) Listen ahead of time and get your parts in order, but also be prepared to play, or at least be familiar with, the other parts you haven't been asked to! This way if things change, you can **adapt!**" - Sam Kennedy (Jess Glynne, Foxes, John **Newman**)

"Different positions will require different levels of player depending on the requirements, but generally, I'd be looking for an exceptional player at their given instrument. If they haven't got any past credits or experience within the field, that's definitely not a deal breaker. However, I would have to trust that they can get the job done and more so, somebody who is working as a full time musician already would be more preferable.

I also really look for somebody who is unique. A lot of higher education music schools will churn out carbon copies of the same player, all believing that because they are a certain way, it will make them more employable. I can only speak from personal experience, but when I'm watching a gig, there's nothing more inspiring than seeing band members with a THING. What I mean by that is a flair, an individuality that elevates the performance rather than a guy in black at the back of the stage soullessly playing the parts. A good band is the sum of its parts, and when you have awesome individual parts that compliment each other and the artist, you're on to a winner." - **PD**

Be Self Sufficient

"As with all session musician's, you need to be self sufficient – bring your own gear and make sure it is of good quality! Don't turn up assuming everything will be ok on the day – even small things like guitarists with pedal boards forgetting extension cables and requiring one from the venue. Keyboard players without suitable stands for more than one piano at a time. Check ahead of time with the MD regarding your gear - tell them what you have and they will likely green light you or advise you on what else you may need. It sounds obvious, but these are things that really go against you. If you turn up to rehearsal and you have a very slick, tidy, self contained rig, where everything just comes out the box and it's set up in minutes where all you're saying is "I just need a plug socket" - that is the dream really and a very good first impression.

A note for guitarists and bassists – be realistic...We are not gonna be touring your 4x12 cab! It's actually pretty unusual for guitarists to be using amps on smaller gigs anyway. Usually you will just be DI'd, so make sure you have a good DI or Emulator for your sounds and tones. Alternatively have a smaller amp like a Fender Princeton...change the speakers in it so it sounds good. Don't rock up to a gig with just a pedal board expecting to plug into a house amp as your sound is going to be different every time. All of these factors add to being self contained unit and thus more employable!" - **SK**

Playability and Gear covered; Next on the agenda is:

Image; This comes in two forms – attire and personality.

"There's that typical session player look which is black skinny's, boots, a long black Tee and a leather jacket – This by default is the stereotypical session outfit. But, it's a good look because it's safe.

You're not offending anyone by wearing a bright orange tee shirt with pink trainers and taking the attention away from the artist, which I think is an important mentality to have. You need to be able to blend in 90% of the time, causing no fuss, problems or having any big opinions, but when you get on stage you need to look slick and perform with lots of energy. I'm looking for session players who realise it's not about them – it's about the project, it's about the artist." - **SK**

"Physical appearance will matter solely on what the artist is looking for. There's no one size fits all answer for this topic, however, being in good physical shape, having a good haircut and dress sense will help you in most pop music outfits.

For me, your personality is on a par with your playing ability in terms of importance. There are 24 hours in every day and you're probably only going to be playing for a maximum of 3 of them. This means there is a lot of time spent sitting around passing time, whether in a van, or a car or bus. For me, finding people that will fit together personally is as important as musically. Vibe is everything on a tour and cohesion is key. Be nice, open, keen to work hard, trustworthy but most importantly – honest." - **PD**

I've had players before who's ego has been greater of that of the artist and they've obviously been sacked as that is not what we want. It's not about you and your guitar solo; It's about coming in and playing the correct parts, being nice and polite, asking lots of questions about other people, rather than just telling everyone about your gear and parts and ideas. So from a personality point of view – we are looking for people who are very charming, very nice, very humble, honest and agreeable. Leave ego's at the door and enter with your understated cool look!" - **Anon**

Money and Rates

"Here's an interesting point; There is such a thing as the **125 club** – a phrase coined between a few people over the past 10 or so years and that is the <u>perception of how much a player is worth</u>; There are lots of fantastic players who are brilliant musicians, but they never get booked because in my eyes or in the eyes of others, you don't really want to book a player who is going out for £125 a day - they're just a bit too cheap for the project.

Believe it or not, the rate you set yourself will define your ability to have a successful career and will affect you image. If you start your career at £100 a day, you will spend the next 5 years struggling to get it up to £200. You can dream of going from £100 to £300, but I think there is a certain perception that if you are on a solid day rate, which these days is probably £250, your reputation just looks better and more attractive to an MD.

If you had the option to choose someone who is a good player and has been working successfully on a proper day rate, opposed to someone who has been going out for £75-100 for a long time, you are more likely to choose the more professional on paper. It sounds horrible, but it's the truth and I'm just being honest. The 125 club may be full of great players, but it's players who have set a bad example.

I think one of the greatest frustrations as an MD is organising rates for musician's. Obviously, I want a great rate and I want my band members to be on a great rate. I'm usually quite open with how much money I'm earning with my band members, because ultimately I'm responsible for the budget. If I say to them "I'm really sorry, there's not enough money in this budget for us all to be on

£300 flat a day, I'm on X and this is how much money I can get you" - I think that's a very reasonable and honest way of of making people know I'm trying to get them the best fee for the gig." - **Anon**

Rates: Bad Practice

"I think it is a really bad vibe when musician's say "It's fine, we'll go out for £100 a day, that's cool." I think it ruins the ability for others to make a living in music. For all the 20 year olds out there who are happy to play for a signed artist under these conditions, what you're doing is teaching record labels that they can get musicians to just do the job for next to nothing, which devalues their entire career.

If you want to be a session musician into your 30's and 40's, you want to buy a house and have a family, pay your taxes etc. you need to be on a good day rate and you need to be busy! **Agreeing to low rates puts you in a bad bracket, limits your career and makes your life a lot harder**, so when you've stopped having your party lifestyle at £100 a day for however many months or years, you realise you're never going to be able to buy a house because you're not on enough money and because you've been telling your management or label you're happy with free rehearsal or travel days – it's a difficult position to be in.

We've all been there; I started my career (hand on my heart) programming for £75 a day and it was abysmal! I did it because I was super young and I didn't have anybody telling me this - Don't charge that, charge a minimum of £200/250 a day. If I'd known that, I wouldn't have spent the next 5, nearly 7 years, crawling up the ladder trying to get to a sustainable rate. I shot myself in the foot from the beginning and I understand why people do it, but it is a case of education and MD's should be saying to session musicians getting into the game DO NOT GO IN CHEAP." – **Anon**

Am I worth it?

Money is a big talking point in this game, really; Am I worth it? Ultimately you're never going to feel worth the fee you are charging in the beginning, but you somehow need to make yourself believe you are! The fee that you begin with will probably be the fee you are stuck with for a long time.

Negotiation

"Rehearsal days in my opinion should not be a half rate – don't agree to this because they are 10 times as long and require 10 times as much effort. My advice – try to get a flat rate fee, don't work for a half rate rehearsal and you could probably agree a lesser rate for a travel day. The sooner everybody gets on board with this and the sooner the session musicians have the balls to stick to it, the more money everyone is gonna start making.

Sometimes you have to be willing to lose a gig to earn more money – I personally turned down an entire support tour for a HUGE Global Artist because the management decided the band should take a slashed travel day rate, which was completely different from the rates we had originally agreed. So I walked away from the gig and someone else ended up taking my place - but the time I wasn't on it, I ended up MD'ing one of the best artists I've ever worked for, for twice the money, if not 3 times! It just goes to show if you stand up for yourself and you make a bold decision it can benefit you in the long run. I have zero regrets about turning down this tour, when everyone said "You're crazy!". Know your worth, know your value and be confident." **- Anon**

Stay Active

Play other genre's for your own sanity! I think it's very easy to fall into a trap within the pop industry of only playing pop and rock, which could limit your musicianship and take away from the colourful playability you had growing up. Keep your palate of skills wide and diverse.

It is a difficult industry

"Being a session musician is a great life for a finite period of time in my opinion. If you want to see the world, be on TV, radio, be involved in big commercial projects etc. it is great fun. I'm not sure how sustainable it is as a lifestyle choice, however – If you want to keep your relationship in tact or have a family, it can be a tough balance. If you can make it work, you have to get really lucky to earn enough to live comfortably solely on a session musician wage – more often than not you will have to supplement your living with teaching, corporate work, part time jobs…At this point it's probably a good time to note: You will earn WAY MORE MONEY being a successful covers band musician vs. being a session musician in the pop industry, unless you make it into the top 1%. It's important to know the way it is so you set your career up in the right way! " **- SK**

Summary

"As illustrated, there's not a one size fits all answer as to what MD's look for in a band. Something I learnt a long time ago was that you're not going to be right for every single gig or audition that comes your way, so working on everything within your own control is key. Work on playing, style, personality, relationships with other musicians, but most importantly trusting in yourself that if it feels right, you're doing it right. "If You Build It, They Will Come." - **PD**

Money Management

As a freelance musician, you will likely be self employed! This means you have to be responsible for all records of incoming and outgoing monies to your account. You may have a part time job for which you are taxed with PAYE, but the freelance music business is yours alone and it is advisable to register for self employment sooner rather than later. The best option is to become a 'sole trader'.

It may seem daunting, but registering this way can give you a real sense of pride in your business. You are responsible for yourself, generating your own income for your own business!

Some people, myself included, opt to have an accountant file your yearly tax returns; They are professionals at what they do, so I don't see how I could do it better by struggling through a tax form.

That being said, a lot of musicians do opt to complete these yearly returns themselves. It can save on accountant's fees, but unless you know what you're doing and what you (legally) can claim for, it may cost you more money in tax in the long run.

What does 'claiming' mean?

As per any business, you are going to have **expenses**. For instance, let's say you have a one off gig that's paying you £200 for the night; You have to drive there, so you have to fill up your car with £20. You then arrive at the gig to find you have to pay for parking – another £5. Then you discover there's no food at the gig *(This is turning into a shocker of a gig by the looks of things)*, so you go and buy some dinner at £10; That is £35 that you have just spent from your total fee, leaving you with £165 – would it seem fair if the government then taxed you on the full £200, even though you only took home £165? Of course not. Now imagine doing this 3-5 times a week at home or for 6 weeks on tour...it's a LOT of expenditure.

(On top of this you will also have to pay a yearly car tax, MOT and parking permit - if you live in london or other big cities)

These are your expenses and they will mount up over the course of a year, so to save yourself money in the long run, you must keep an accurate record. The best way to do this is keeping physical receipts for EVERYTHING you think is claimable. I also like to use a spreadsheet to update my monthly income / expenditure and then forward these on to my accountant. It's better than just handing her a jumbled bag of receipts! It is also important to have for your own records.

What is claimable?

As I mentioned above, this is why I pay my accountant. However, I will try my best to break things down into sections. Everything you purchase when you are 'at work' or for work (instruments, accessories, stage clothes etc.) should be deductible to an extent. Below is a list of how my expenses are broken down.

- Travel & Subsistence – petrol, cab fares, food, parking etc.
- Clothing & Laundry – if you buy clothes to wear on stage or use laundering services on tour.
- Bank Charges
- Postage & Stationary – do you sell online products that you have to ship?
- Insurance – Instruments, travel, car, home & contents etc.
- Research
- Repairs, Consumables – car (MOT, servicing, maintenance), instruments, electronics.
- Promotion, Subscription – Streaming services (Spotify/Apple Music), website, advertising your services etc.

- Accountancy, Admin – In my case, my accountant's charges.
- Telephone, Fax, Internet – We are running a business and need to use these to survive
- Use of home studio – Do you work from home? Recording, emailing, writing, researching - Some of your rent will be deductible

If you are reading this thinking "I don't use half of those things and I don't want to risk being taxed as self employed before I earn enough!" - Don't worry! The current tax threshold is £12,500, meaning anything you earn under this per year will not be taxable. It is still good practice to be registered and not pay, rather than run the risk of earning under the radar. For my first few years of self employment, I paid no tax due to not earning enough or my accountant being able to deduct enough expenses to put me under the threshold.

An example in simple terms:

If I earn £18,000 a year from music, but my expenses come in at £6,000, it only leaves me with £12,000 worth of taxable income – this falls under the threshold, so no tax is due.

Ross's whirlwind crash-course in accounting complete, The Musician's Union (https://bit.ly/2t8tLY6) has some great advice on their website and can do a better job of explaining the finer details!

Invoicing

Again, the staple for any professional musician! Whenever you agree a fee for a gig and wish to get paid - 90% of the time, you will have to send an invoice to the person who booked you. An Invoice is defined simply as *'a list of goods sent or services provided, with a statement of the sum due for these; a bill.'*

The best thing to do is create a template on your phone/computer that has all your basic details pre-saved; Name, Address, Bank Details (both Domestic & International – IBAN / SWIFT) etc. This way whenever you fill in your 'customers' details it is fast and efficient and less mistakes are likely to happen. If you pay for an app like QuickBooks, it will save all your previous invoices and contacts, which is great if you gig regularly with the same people. It also makes it a lot easier when it comes time to fill in your yearly accounts.

Invoices, by UK law, generally get paid within 30 days. Of course, if this was the case being self employed would be easy! I have had to chase countless invoices that have arrived 1,2..sometimes 4 months late. I spoke to a friend the other day who told me one (well known) artist failed to pay her band for 7 months! This is just one of the stresses of being self employed, but generally people will pay you in good time.

If a situation like this does arise, you are entitled to charge an interest rate on late payments, however, it is not good practice to enforce this unless somebody is really taking the proverbial out of you! If they are ignoring your emails or calls and no payment date or excuse has been offered to you, you could proceed with it – but be aware this will likely be the last time you will be offered work from this party – then again, if they aren't paying you, a good question would be "Why do I want to work for this person again?"

A good addition to any invoice suggested by the government to deter late payments is the following:

"We understand and will exercise our statutory right to claim interest and compensation for debt recovery costs under the late payment legislation if we are not paid according to agreed credit terms"

Business you and Personal you

It is advisable to set up a separate bank account that you use solely for business transactions; Number one being the receipt of all monies generated from music, but also equipment purchases, insurance, streaming services, day to day work expenses (petrol / food) etc. If this is your sole income, you will also need to pay yourself a wage into your everyday account that you use for personal purchases (when you're not 'at work'). This is also when you start to see the separation between your business and *you* as mentioned earlier in our mental health section.

I recently listened to a great podcast by entrepreneur, business coach and former musician, Graham Cochrane, who talks about 'money management for small businesses'. It's on Spotify and I'd recommend everyone who wants to set themselves up correctly as a successful business to check it out.

A quick rundown of his tips:

1) **Have a separate business bank account!** This is for 'business' you

2) **Calculate your monthly business expenses** so you know how much money you NEED to generate every month to be profitable.

3) **Calculate your tax** percentage and move this into a separate business account (20% if you earn between £12,501-£50,000). This way you stay on top of what you owe!

4) **Pay yourself a salary that you can afford** every month! As a business owner you are both employer and employee, so you have to commit to a salary every month that you pay into your employee's personal bank account.

5) **Don't use your business account as a piggy bank!** It's easy to fool yourself that if you have a good business month, you can treat yourself to some of the extra profit

and pay yourself more; As a self employed business you will have good months and bad months, so in order to create and maintain a sustainable career, you have to commit to the same salary you've defined in point 3 above. If your business earned £5,000 a month, as an employer you wouldn't pay your employee £4,000 a month, would you?

6) **Extra Profit;** Your goal should be to try and save a minimum of 10% profit a month after expenses and salary and set it aside in a savings account. Alternatively, you can flip this and put profit first, followed by expenses and salary, but only if you can afford to do so. Your goal is to get ahead!

7) **Build cash reserves with this profit** to avoid living pay-check to pay-check. Revenue is inconsistent, but expenses are fixed, so we have to prepare. This way if we need to 'borrow' money to stay afloat, we do it from ourselves in the form of a loan.

It is important to set yourself up correctly, so you can enjoy the creative side of music that we all enjoy. If you put these measures in place early on, it will allow you to see how your business is thriving and plan for the future to maintain a (hopefully) long and successful career!

Support Slots

Support slots are a great way to engage a brand new audience for the first time, but how do you put yourself in the position to land yourself one?

One option is to approach artists directly. As daft as it may sound, this is sometimes the easiest and best method; I've seen first hand 2 artists I work for secure some of the biggest support slots in the world – One was for TwentyOnePilots, the other was Ed Sheeran!

Don't get me wrong – this is not an everyday occurrence and a lot of right place at the right time was involved. However, saying that, you could put yourself in the right place, at the right time! Look at your local listings to see which bands are coming through and if they have announced support yet - If they haven't, there may be an opportunity, so there is no harm in trying to get in touch! If you can't get a band contact, try their booking agent – this will be one of the easier contacts to find...it's how bands make their money!

Make sure you stand out from the crowd – what separates you from all the other bands trying to secure this slot? Ask yourself what you can bring to the show – do you have lots of local fans you can bring? Can you hype the crowd? Do you fit within the same genre? Having a clear selling point will help you get in with right people.

Alternatively, try to get a good reputation with local promoters and create a bit of a buzz about your product; If a band comes to town and uses a local promoter, they may be given the responsibility for sourcing the support, so it helps if you have a good relationship and are one of the stand out acts.

If you have landed a support slot on a tour, try to create as little of a footprint as possible. By this I mean be a self-contained unit. Don't rely on the headline artist or their team for anything...they have enough on their plate without your burdens. This isn't to say they won't help, but don't assume!

Make your setup as simple as possible! Some days you might only get a 15 minute soundcheck because of the headliner's technical issues or set changes - You don't want your whole set to be put in jeopardy because of a complicated set up.

Ask the stagehands in advance where to stack your gear after your set and try to case it up as soon as possible to avoid loss or breakages. Don't go off socialising until all of your gear is taken care of – it will be the single quickest way to annoy everyone.

Remember this is an incredible opportunity to win a new fan base. Be nice to the headliner – thank them for having you on their tour and be sincere. Do your research - Learn about them and their product...why they've gotten to where they are. This will at least give you some insight into their fans and how you can win them over.

Be organised with **merchandise** – it is one of, if not the strongest form of income on a tour - I have seen negative deficit tours saved by it. Be creative and price it fairly. Make sure you have a varied amount of products and try to tie it in with your tour ethos. Sales will be further driven if you sell yourself – the fans want to meet you, so get out on that stall and sell after your performance!

Promote yourself during your set and include the audience – try sing alongs or get them to clap different rhythms. The fans are all there because they love music, so challenge them! It will make for a much more memorable experience. Mention your name more than once and talk about your new material, where to find it and when they can see you next - Lots of support slots are lined up in conjunction with a following headline tour...it is the best promotion, so be sure to book a local show ASAP!

Shout out the headliner during your set and they will likely do the same in theirs! It equates to more promotion and it hypes the crowd – everyone's a winner!

Quick-fire Questions

Recently I reached out the musical public to find out the real questions that people wanted to know the answers to. These answers themselves will likely generate more questions as a result, so please feel free to ask more to me at rosscraibdrums.com.

"How do you play the same songs over 100 times without hating them?" - Kinley

This is the great thing about working with musicians and artists you love – if you enjoy the music, you will rarely get tired of playing it. That is one of the biggest bits of advice I could give for any musician – play music you enjoy and that makes you fulfilled.

When you play a song live to a new group of people...the feeling becomes new again. Looking into the crowd and seeing how that song relates to them and how special it can be, you share an experience rather than just the bare bones of the song.

Don't get me wrong, rehearsing a song over and over can become quite repetitive and tedious, but if you've chosen music as a career, you have to understand every day isn't a breeze and a party; These are the bits of hard work behind the scenes that allow you to feel comfortable on stage and really enjoy the special parts of being a performer.

"How does it affect you if you mess up live?"

This is an interesting question; The best thing about music is when you watch it, listen to it, play it in a gig scenario – It's live!...it will never be EXACTLY the same again and that's what makes it special for the players and the audience.

Yes, you will be playing identical parts, but the way in which you choose to play them at any given moment can fluctuate based on your surroundings; Maybe another musician on stage will play a lick, sing a certain phrase differently or even make a mistake which you feel would be complimented by you changing your part to suit. Therein lies the beauty of live music. It's all about chemistry between the people on stage and in the audience.

As I mentioned in the mental health section, you will always be your own worst critic! It will always be way worse in your head than it appears to the audience, because they don't know the song arrangement inside-out like you do. What can feel like an eternity for you is just a fleeting moment for them that they might not even understand!

That said, if you do make a mistake, try to brush it off...it's happened and it's already in the past! The worst thing you can do is dwell on it for the rest of the show which will only hinder your otherwise enjoyable performance. When we play live and somebody makes a little mistake, we just laugh it off – sometimes other band members won't even notice! But in laughing it off, the audience will see you having fun and just go along with it. Laughter and happiness is infectious and a good vibe at a concert fills the room, and leaves a much stronger lasting memory and feeling than that one bum note. It also helps the musician who messed up feel comfortable again and settle back into the set with no judgement.

You're only human after all!

"How important is music theory? Is knowing the technical part of playing an instrument enough or does knowing the deep intricacies of how music really works, equally essential?" - Falguni

Theory is not essential to become a good player or songwriter, however, technique combined with knowledge and theory really just allows you to expand your vocabulary as a musician, allowing you to write better songs or parts with more freedom and without so many limitations.

You will understand the 'why's' a lot more in certain styles of music and it will help you feel a lot more comfortable when working with other musicians. As a drummer, my musical theory isn't as strong as someone who plays a melodic instrument like keys or guitar, but understanding the chords and harmonies of a song just helps...and it makes it a lot more fun! That being said, I will likely have stronger attributes in other areas – it depends what direction you wish to go really.

I always think learning more throughout your journey is key...you should never just settle for not knowing, but at the same time, don't let it stop you; Your time, sound and feel are the ultimate attributes to what makes the core of music sound good – the rest is just added musicianship.

How do you memorize easiest?

This varies for me based on how complex the song is. Fortunately drums and percussion parts can be quite repetitive per section, so you may only be learning 4 different parts for the whole song.

Usually, I'll write out the structure and put a few little notes beside each section. See below an example.

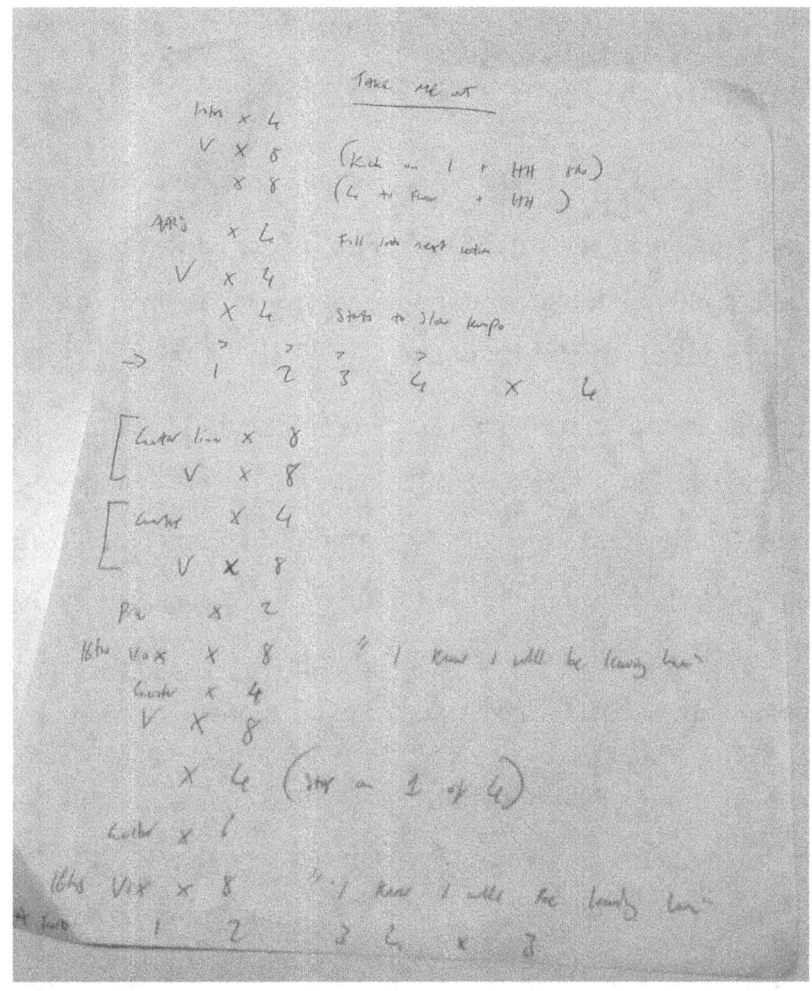

Take Me Out by Franz Ferdinand

I then work through each section's basic grooves without the music until comfortable, eventually playing through it to get a feel. Then I'll dive a little deeper to really pick out the little inflictions that make the groove complete. Then it's just a matter of repetition until I'm comfortable.

Little things that help me are the vocals and lyrics and certain chords or key changes. The more details you know of the song, the better!

"Have you ever been full of self doubt / fear while on tour; Not feeling good or talented enough compared to everyone else around you? If so, how do you cope with it? - Claire

I think most musicians would be lying if they said at some point they haven't felt a sense of self doubt; It is very common! It's otherwise known as 'imposter syndrome' and anyone who finds themselves under some form of microscope (on stage for instance) will have likely suffered it at some point. It is essentially the fear of being exposed as a 'fraud' and not good enough.

I've even struggled with it whilst writing the content for this book! You ask yourself, "what gives me the right to offer this information?" or "why do I deserve to be in this position?...I'm not an *expert*!"

The way to deal with it is to just accept that you are valuable and you do deserve to be in this position due to hard work and improvement. If you are a songwriter or creator – just look back at some of the first content you created...you'll probably cringe at the thought of it, but you can use this as a motivator to see how far you've come in your journey.

Speak to people you trust to vent your worries – chances are they will have been in a similar situation in their lives or career. The sooner you realise most of the world is living under the 'fake it 'til you make it' motto, you will no longer feel alone or in over your head.

You don't have to be an "expert" to feel like you can offer value to other people's lives – just ask yourself - "will this help somebody?"

And rather than thinking on a global scale about the masses of people; Instead think - "will my friend's like it?".

Life is a journey and if you can help somebody along the way, whether it be through music or content or advice, you are offering value and you no longer need to feel fear or self-doubt!

Working with musicians you consider more talented than yourself should also encourage and push you to become better! It will elevate your playing and this should be a positive, not a negative – Don't be intimidated...instead embrace it and learn!

"Is it hard grounding yourself when moving between cities all the time? Do you have any techniques you've feel have helped to stop yourself going crazy and feeling all over the place?" - Katie

Routine is key on tour...and it's actually a lot more structured than you may think. I actually feel more of a sense of routine on tour than I do back home!

For example, soundcheck will be at the same time most days...as will stage time; Therefore, so will lunch and dinner (give or take a few hours)....this just leaves you the times in between to enjoy the beautiful cities you find yourself in!

Some of the guys on tour go running every morning or discover local coffee shops. Again this is a nice way to see a city and get a bit of normality every day!

It can get a little chaotic and some days you will miss a taste of normality if you are far from home in a different cultured city, but I just remember one of my reasons for pursuing music – I wanted to see the world and experience new things, so you learn to embrace it!

Your tour family also ground you; If you are lucky like me to find a great bunch of friends who share similar values, who you enjoy spending time with, the feeling of 'home' is never too far away!

"How does everyone *really* feel about meeting fans afterwards? Are y'all happy to meet us, or are you so tired you just want to get in the bus and go to sleep?" - Hailee

We never take fans for granted; You guys are the reason we are able to visit all of these beautiful places and we love meeting you and hearing your stories! You make the shows as special for us as (hopefully) we do for you!

All I would say is: tours are long and there will be some days we may be feeling a little tired or run down and just not really up to meeting new people, but that is no reflection on the fans themselves.

"How do we get our foot in the door of opportunity and what kind of opportunities should I take to make that step efficient?" - Layna

The biggest asset you can accumulate over your career is contacts! As I mentioned in Chapter 5, Networking is key to gaining the most organic relationships and cultivating opportunities. There is no golden bullet to getting an opportunity, as they can arise from the craziest of places or encounters.

All I would say when starting out is take every opportunity that comes your way (to an extent); You never know who you may meet on a gig, event or social gathering. The most successful musicians I know are all great in social scenarios as it is where your personality shines; People want to work with great people first and foremost before a note is even played!

Take risks, reach out to people, collaborate and don't be scared to share your material. One of the most crippling things is perfectionism – some people, myself included, will keep working on something until they feel it is perfect, but ultimately it never will be; Get your content out there and share it...it's the only way people will know what you are up to!

Put yourself in a good position by meeting as many people in your field, in your area as possible! If your music falls within a certain genre, go to gigs and meet like-minded fans. Build relationships with industry contacts or other musician's on a similar level as you.

"How can I get a band together that are all musically experienced and will help compose different musical elements of my songs whilst still being broke?"

This is a bit of a catch-22, as the experienced players will likely want...and deserved to be paid for their hard work. If money is a real issue, try to find it first before you commit to finding a great band or alternatively start a band, where you split all the income and writing down the middle. This will mean everyone is invested from the beginning and an equal partner. If you wish to go down the solo artist route, read **Orla Gartland's** advice in our 'Tips from the Pro's' section about how to succeed as an independent artist.

"Do I have to have music online somewhere for venues to book me? How do I contact venues to book shows and can I ask the venue to have me as support for touring artists or do I have to go directly to the artist / management?" - Mimi

This is quite a vast question which I have covered lots of in chapter 6, but regards music online;

Music online I'd say is pretty essential; You may not have it released to the public, but having a private Soundcloud link with at least 2 or 3 demo's will need to exist to grab industry attention; You can't just approach someone asking for a gig if they have never heard your material – it's just too much of a risk for promoters.

Regards getting support slots – Chapter 7 has the answers!

"How do I approach the idea of recording demos for Soundcloud with no knowledge?"

As a follow on to the above answer; You will need to have knowledge of recording softwares or 'DAW's', such as Logic or Pro Tools; These are the platforms that will record your music into in order to edit and produce. This is the most cost effective way of recording demo's.

However, if you don't know how to work these systems, you will need to source the services of a music producer. You can do this either by collaborating, potentially sharing writing credits on a song, or alternatively paying for a more established producer. If you are going down this route, do your research – try to pick producers who specialise in the genre you are aiming for or who have worked with artists you aspire to sound like.

In today's industry, it is important that the music you release or use to represent yourself is of a high enough quality; The market is so flooded and with a lot of competition, you need to do what you can to stand out from the rest of the crowd. If you do get your chance and someone influential listens to your demo's, you need to be confident in the quality of them.

It can be more costly up front employing good musicians and producers to work / play on your tracks, but it really will stand you in good stead moving forwards in your career.

"I've been struggling with not feeling good or talented enough to play music, and I feel like if I can't do or play something perfectly the first time, then I might as well not be doing it at all. Do you have any advice on how to overcome that perfectionism?" - Olivia

Music is a discipline; It takes time and lots of hard work to get to a stage where we can feel competent or good enough that we can speak 'the language' without feeling too restricted in your so called 'vocabulary.'

There is such a thing called muscle memory; When you are playing an instrument with difficult techniques you need to practice in order to train your brain to do this more naturally – the more you practice it, the more natural it will feel and come to you. Your muscles will remember the motion and therefore perform the task more effortlessly.

I guess what I'm saying is – nothing will be perfect the first time as you have to train your brain to correspond to the muscular movements needed to gain the result you are trying to achieve, whether it be on a guitar, your voice or a drum kit etc. The same can be said for many aspects of your life – languages / reading & writing / sports etc.

We've all been there before and will most definitely be there again. Boundaries will continue to be hit and in order to become a better musician, we need to find ways to overcome them, without fixating too much on the failure aspect – look at it as a challenge and you will feel the rewards when you break through undoubtedly in the end.

For you, what are some ways in which you feel you add value to the people around you and to your own personal development while on and off tour? - Ash

A great, deep question here from Ash and one that leads me to question myself a little bit! We touched on imposter syndrome earlier and having to analyse myself I find those thoughts creeping back in.... "How *do* I add value?"...

I guess I'll start with my personality type! I like to think of myself as quite a positive person and with the dodie team being into their Enneagram types, they have labelled me a number 7;

An Enneagram crash course for those in the dark - It is essentially a personality test with 9 different personality *types*, one of which will suit you best. Of course, there will be aspects of all *types* within your personality, however, one will stand out beyond the rest; Number 7 for me – The Enthusiast.

Simplified, a Number 7 is defined as "The Busy, Fun-Loving Type: Spontaneous, Versatile, Distractible, and Scattered".

On tour I like to make sure everyone is happy, included and up for a good time! I like to be a shoulder to cry on and offer a comfortable place for people to trust in me and come to me with any problems they may be having, whilst offering some caring advice.

In regards my own development, I feel there is always room for improvement...

One thing I've noticed / been told - I bottle up a lot of tension or emotions whilst on the road for the benefit of those around me; In other words I don't let it show if I'm having a bad day or feeling a bit blue for whatever reason. I feel like I will bring the mood down if I open up, so therefore I keep it hidden. I know this is a negative or backwards step in my personality growth, so I'm working at opening up a little more.

The ways in which I add value to myself – I like to experience new things everywhere I go with an open mind, look to other cultures for things I can implement into my own life back home, get creative and inspired by those I meet and continue to try being a better human all round. I don't like just sitting still in life and I'm always looking for inspiration in ways I can further my own personal growth, whilst maintaining a good reputation and friendships along the way.

I hope that kind of answered that question....

"When not on tour, how do you personally sustain yourself? E.g Teaching, Session Recordings, Corporate gigs, online services." - Dom

To be honest, all of the above in some form or other! I've had a LOT of different jobs in my time, but I think the key is to always be moving forwards and have lots of sources of income.

When I first graduated from University, I was lucky enough to get a job teaching drums as part of a music service. Don't get me wrong, the money wasn't great and I had no previous knowledge of how to interact with kids, never mind teach them, but what it did do was allow me to learn; I watched how others worked and I learnt the business side behind the scenes. I managed to amass a pool of around 40 students per week and gain a good reputation with the parents and heads of music in each school; Through the contacts I met, I was then offered my own school with my own private students away from the music service. This meant my income nearly tripled and I became my own boss. This was around

5 years ago and now I work on my own terms and around my schedule picking up lessons as and where I choose. I essentially run my own music service now by paying teachers to cover my lessons and taking a fee for my organisation.

The more you play in a city, the more gigs you will get offered; Another staple income for a session musician is function work with covers bands – weddings, corporate events, birthdays etc. If you get in with some good bands and agencies, you can make upwards of £250 per gig...these can add up per week and you can make loads of new contacts - which can lead to more exciting opportunities, such as the pop gigs we all want!

It's not quite as glamorous as playing in front of 3,000 every night, but the money is good and the better the band you play for, the more interesting events you will play – this will still allow you to travel and see the world and offer you a bit of security in the touring downtime. I currently play for around 8 different covers bands when I'm in London, which obviously is a huge pool of musicians, and quite a sustainable number of gigs per year. Of course there are diary clashes, but it allows me to choose the best gig for my needs.

It is important to budget yourself per month! Touring is where most musicians will make a chunk of their yearly income, especially if you tour for long periods of time. As discussed in the business section, the best thing to do is to allocate yourself a monthly wage which will allow you to make that bigger chunk of money last in downtimes or go towards savings.

Session recordings of course are good forms of income too, however with the modern day softwares, it's becoming increasingly less common and you'd be lucky to survive solely on these. The best advice would be to get in with a good, busy producer who likes what you do; That way when they get artists through the door who need instrumentation, you are their first port of call!

Write your own music! This can be library music, for sync, or just writing sessions with other artists; I receive quarterly income from PRS for tracks that I have written and have been played on radio or performed live. If you get some national play-listing it can be very lucrative.

PPL (the credit for performing on a track) will also generate a quarterly income, however this pays significantly less than PRS (the writing credits).

Run your own band; I play in another originals project called Circumnavigate – A Scandi-Folk project who have had some success in sync by securing a few US film placements. These can be quite lucrative, with the added bonuses of merchandise, gig fees, festival appearances etc. However, this is probably the most difficult form of income!

These are my main forms of income at present, however, I'm currently looking at branching out into more business based services and investments. As mentioned it's good to think outside the box and not restrict yourself solely within the confines of music – Use it to get in and get ahead, but then look elsewhere for opportunity and try to cross over where possible!

Advice from the Pro's

I know how these things go – why should you listen to me ramble on for 90+ pages when there's so many different angles and points of view of tour life?

As an addition to the public's questions, I felt I should bring in a selection of my talented friends with some words of advice!

John Bird Jr.

(Niall Horan, Jack Savoretti)

Photo by Christian Tierney

You've toured the world for 2 years with one of the world's biggest stars, Niall Horan. How do you survive being away from home for that long?

"Being away from home is the hardest part of the job – not just during the times you are away, but also when you are home trying to readjust to day to day life. The phone stops ringing because you've been out of the loop for so long, both with friends and work.

I guess you just have to put extra effort keeping in contact with people and making time to see them on the road – putting them on the guest list is not enough!

Speak to the guys on tour with you – everyone is going through the same thing, missing family and friends, so share the load.

Also, for yourself, try to do something daily that you would continue both on and off the road! Something that creates a balance between the 2 worlds. Whether it's a hobby or even going to the gym. It can keep one thing constant even when your routine keeps changing. This will help you to feel grounded."

Matt Greig

(Jessie J, Daniel Caesar, Jordan Rakei)

photo by Travis Poston

What do FOH engineers like to see from their musicians on stage?

"The most important part of the relationship between the FOH engineer and musicians on stage is willingness on both ends to be flexible when it comes to making decisions. If something needs to be changed, I.E cab volume, tunings etc. then it is important to open a dialogue and work together to find a solution if something is wrong. A lot of musicians are unwilling to make any changes at all, as it may push them outside of their comfort zone; This is sometimes justified, but if they are open to the idea of change and thinking about the problem from an audio perspective, the show will always benefit."

dodie

(With more than 100 million Spotify streams and 3 EP's which have charted in the UK, US Billboard & Australian album charts, dodie is a self-made superstar)

Photo by Rena Lexantiago

How do you deal with mental health on tour and what are the keys to staying happy?

"Learn to share to the group if you're feeling particularly rough one day. Your tour crew are your family, and they'll be able to sense if you're feeling down and just trying to get on anyway. People like to help when they can! You'll hopefully get a few shoulders to cry on and extra cups of tea made for you."

Orla Gartland

(With half a million monthly listeners, Orla has led the way in demonstrating how successful independent artists can become in today's industry.)
Photo by Stevie Kyle

Any tips for independent artists wanting to put on their own headline shows or tours?

What struggles or pitfalls should they watch out for?

"Touring and gigging as an independent solo artist can be tough but so, so rewarding when you pull it off. Keep your team tight -

find people who love your music & will double up on jobs when they can. My MD (the perfect Pete Daynes) can also drive, my all-round sound wizard, Conor Cosimini, helps us set our monitor mixes during soundcheck and then jumps on front of house for the show.

Educate yourself on the various roles within the live side of the music industry - particularly promoters & booking agents. You don't need either on board at first to begin playing shows - start out by looking for support slots from friends or cold emailing the teams around artists who are currently touring. If you're the right fit up you could be exposed to rooms full of new potential fans of your music, build up some essential live skills and eventually grow enough demand to put on a headline show of your own.

Be transparent with and fair to those who work with you - everyone starts somewhere and most people will understand if you have to keep the fees at a modest rate to begin with. Just make it clear that they'll increase as you progress & don't take advantage of anyone - over time it can feel discouraging. When you have a bunch of hired hands on board it's absolutely normal for your show to cost more to put on than you'll be paid to play, but if you want an amazing show you need amazing people, and they deserve to be paid fairly. So suck it up and find the money somewhere!"

Liam Patrick Cromby

(We Are The Ocean)

photo by Angelah Betmead

You've toured he world as part of the same band for 10 years. How did you survive for so long?

"From the beginning to the end a band life is like a family. Through the ups and downs, we always pulled through together. Communication is key!"

Anna Andresdotter Nilsson

(Booking Agent)

photo by Napsugar Bardocz

What can bands or artists do to entice booking agents to check them out and take them more seriously?

"The most obvious and straight on answer must be: talent and good songs. However, there is much more than this that goes into an agent taking on or noticing an artist.

Agents are in constant contact with the rest of the music industry; They get recommendations from managers, promoters and labels all the time, so they will take this much more into account than if they receive an email directly from a band...to be quite honest, the latter will probably get ignored. They will have a listen to that secret Soundcloud link or any songs the artist has released, but most likely will move on if they're not hooked within the first 20 seconds. They are busy people with very little time to spare on their hands. Remember that when you're sending your approach - don't be cliché or make the pitch too long!

Other things Agents will take in to account are the similarities to other artists, but obviously without being exactly the same. Think Sam Smith, Lewis Capaldi and Adele for example - they all have very sad songs but are hilarious as people. Social media following and streaming numbers; they take into account. If the artist has a record label, management company and what the team is behind them. If there is previous touring history Agents will want the information of how well these tours performed, ticket sales etc.

You don't have to fit within a specific genre - find your gap in the market...your people. That will get you the industry attention you're after.

Once you have managed to get an agent down to your gig, make sure you put on a kick ass show and most definitely put your personality forward. No Agent will sign an artist that can't entertain a crowd...They are live booking agents after all!"

Sophie Emmeline English

(Sam Smith, Jess Glynne, Rag 'n' Bone Man)

photo by Stevie Kyle

What attributes do classical players need to succeed in the pop industry?

Is there a crossover?

"There is certainly a crossover between the classical and pop industry, which is why so many classically trained musicians work in the pop world! There are several useful skills, such as being able to arrange parts, fix other players and an ability to be flexible!

No two gigs are the same; You could be in a recording session one day, on stage the next and come the weekend, you might be questioning whether or not you have the X Factor live on TV. Get comfortable with adapting from gig to gig and develop an understanding of what each project requires of you! Some days you'll need to use the skills you refined in your classical training, whilst on others the ability to collaborate with an artist is far more useful.

Lastly, be humble enough to quickly work out your role within each project; Whilst one might require you to take on more of a leading part, the ability to sit back and play with an ensemble is essential."

Charlie Fowler

(Kylie Minogue, Jennifer Hudson, Mahalia)

photo by Silje Forbes

Having worked for many major artists, what advice would you give to younger session musicians just starting out?

"Play as much as possible! Every gig you do play, go in as prepared as you possibly can be... even learn other peoples parts.

Make sure you have the right gear; This can change depending on the gig, but it's important that your sound is right from the get-go.

This may sound like a given but its one of the first things an MD will scrutinise you for, so make sure you have put the time in.

Utilise your other musicians! As an MD you are in charge and its important to have a clear idea of where you're taking the show, but use the experience and knowledge of your musicians to see if they can hear something in an arrangement that you haven't...or perhaps a different way of playing a certain part.

Be kind and listen, ask people questions. There is nothing more flattering than asking someone what they think or how would they do something. In the same breath be confident and play strong."

George Baker

(Songwriter & Producer Manager)

TMS (Grammy Nominated), Joe Kearns (Ellie Goulding),

Phil Cook (Lewis Capaldi)

What makes a good songwriter and what can they do to progress in the industry?

"For me, in this business, it always comes back to the power of a song; Behind every successful artist or huge international record, it ultimately comes down to the songwriting and those behind it who devote their lives to perfecting their craft. Broadly speaking, the greatest writers out there are those that have a knack of dialling into something with universal appeal and connecting with the masses. When you go searching for what makes a 'hit song' or help you connect with a song in particular, people often put this down to a clever lyric, a melodic or instrumental hook or, most of the time, a combination of all of the above. I find that generally the most exciting and successful songwriters out there have their own unique way of presenting things, putting a spin or more distinct touch on what otherwise appears to be like any other pop song. The ability to draw on various influences and references is also crucial. More often than not, when we hear a song, we relate to what we already know and have heard before and the most intelligent writers have the innate ability to do play on a combination of references and different influences whilst creating something fresh and individual.

In many ways, songwriting is very cyclical, just like fashion and other pockets of culture and society - what goes around will come back around but it is about the reinvention and nuances that occur when it does.

Like many sides to the industry, it's hard to know where to start and then, once you've got started, how do you cut through the noise? Well, collaboration on many levels is at the heart of the business I think, and songwriting, more often than not, epitomises that. Whilst some writers do work alone and everyone is different,

I think it's fair to say that the vast majority of writers collaborate and on a very regular basis. For me, that's probably the best place to start as it'll help you learn, hone your craft, build connections and help move things forward. There is always a point too at which the world needs to hear what you are doing and what you have to say, so find a way of doing that and get what feedback you can - don't be afraid and hide your songs away!

Overall though, I would stress that for me, it's always important to have a point of difference; don't just try and replicate your favourite song or style, always strive to create something new and with a point of difference."

Post Tour

Finishing a tour comes with mixed emotions; You will be happy to return to a sense of normality and those you miss and love back at home. You will be excited to sleep in your own bed and catch up on all those missed episodes of your latest TV binge. You will need plenty of sleep and likely a return to healthier ways.

But there will be a part of you that misses all of it; You will miss your tour family – the faces you have grown so accustomed to seeing every day. You will miss the buzz of stepping out on stage every night to adorning fans...the routines, the lifestyle. This is known as *'post tour blues'* and every touring musician will have had it at some point. You just have to remember tour is like a bubble...a life within itself. For new beginnings and future tours to look forward to, it must come to an end.

Try to 'cushion' your fall back to reality – use some of that downtime on the road to plan lots of work and fulfil tasks you have been eager to do since being away. I often find I get very inspired being on a successful tour – it makes me hungry to work harder for myself when I get back, so try and throw yourself headfirst into this.

Dealing with this can be challenging, but you have to focus on the positives and understand the correlation between tour life and life back home. They are almost separate entities as the majority of your friend group will never understand – it is a story you will share with your bandmates forever...full of intricacies and in-jokes, ups and downs...and it truly is a wonderful experience!

I read a great article recently from another touring drummer which sums it all up perfectly, so I thought I would end with this:

> *"It's not the parts with the bright lights. It's not the pictures that the fans see on Instagram. It's the real-life moments of real-life people trying to find a meaning in a mobile life. Finding stability in a transient existence; Unconsciously clawing to find ways to detour around the rockstar archetype and just feel like a kid in a band playing with your friends..."*
>
> *Nick Spreigl*
> *'23 Hours: The Life of a Full-Time Touring Musician'*

Photo Credit: Kyle Jones
dodie @ Shepherds Bush Empire (night 2 – 2018)

Conclusion

A lot of the contents in this small e-book may seem fairly straight forward and obvious, but you'd be surprised how often they are easily overlooked.

If you follow them to a good standard you will make yourself a very employable, well rounded & knowledgable musician in today's hectic, ever-changing music industry.

With this knowledge you can go into a tour feeling confident with awareness of the different relationships and situations you may find yourself in.

I wish you all the best in your career and hope we cross paths one day!

Thank you for your trust and your time,

Ross x

Thank You

A HUGE thank you to everyone who has and is continuing to make this book a reality!

Family, Friends, Colleagues & Acquaintances – I love you all!

To all my contributors – I couldn't have done it without you!

Cover Design: Isra Naseem (IG: @isra.scribbles)

Photographers: Karl Myrvang, Mathew Parri Thomas, Samuel Morris, Stevie Kyle, Christian Tierney, Angelah Betmead, Kyle Jones, Silje Forbes, Napsugar Bardocz, Rena Lexantiago, Travis Poston

Professionals: Pete Daynes, Sam Kennedy, dodie, Orla Gartland, Liam Patrick Cromby, Matt Greig, John Bird Jr., Anna Andresdotter Nilsson, George Baker, Charlie Fowler, Sophie Emmeline English

References

National Heart Lung and Blood Institute. Sleep Deprivation and Deficiency.

Kathleen M. Zelman MPH, RD, LD. What can vitamin C do for your health?

What Should a Musician Eat? (2016) Jesse Sterling Harrison.

Dr. Timothy Jameson (2010) Reach for the Top! The Musician's Guide to Health, Wealth and Success.

UK Music (2017). The contribution of live music to the UK economy.

Broman-Fulks, Joshua & Berman, Mitchell & A Rabian, Brian & Webster, Michael. (2004). Effects of aerobic exercise on anxiety sensitivity. Behaviour research and therapy. 42. 125-36. 10.1016/S0005-7967(03)00103-7.

Noa Kageyama PH.D The Impact of Exercise and Physical Fitness on Performance Under Pressure.

Noa Kakeyama PH.D How to Make Performance Anxiety an Asset Instead of a liability

Nick Spreigl (2016). 23 Hours: The Life of a Full-Time Touring Musician.

Anxiety sensitivity (2014). Harvard Health Publishing. Harvard Medical School.

Sally Anne Gross and Dr. George Musgrave for Help Musicians UK (2016). Can Music Make You Sick? Music and Depression.

Ben Scott (2017) The Seven Deadly Skills.

Musician's Union – Self Assessment.

Sam Skirrow (2018) You are not your business – Pt.1

Lucy Boyle (2016) Is Tequila the New Kombucha?

www.ingramcontent.com/pod-product-compliance
Lightning Source LLC
Chambersburg PA
CBHW071208070526
44584CB00019B/2958